San Luis Obispo

COUNTY

Pictorial Research
by Mark Hall-Patton

Produced in cooperation
with the
San Luis Obispo County
Historical Society

Windsor Publications, Inc.
Chatsworth, California

LOOKING BACKWARD INTO THE
MIDDLE KINGDOM

San Luis Obispo

COUNTY

DANIEL E. KRIEGER

Windsor Publications, Inc.—History Books Division
Managing Editor: Karen Story
Design Director: Alexander D'Anca

Staff for *San Luis Obispo:*
    Looking Backward into the Middle Kingdom
Photo Director: Susan L. Wells
Associate Editor: Jeffrey Reeves
Manuscript Editor: Kim Hogan
Editorial Assistants: Didier Beauvoir, Thelma Fleischer, Kim
    Kievman, Rebecca Kropp, Michael Nugwynne, Kathy B.
    Peyser, Pat Pittman, Theresa J. Solis
Layout Artist, Editorial: Mari Catherine Preimesberger
Designer: Maryanne Gladych

Library of Congress Cataloging-in-Publication Data
Krieger, Daniel E., 1940- San Luis Obispo : Looking Backward
    Into the Middle Kingdom / by Daniel E. Krieger
Pictorial research by Mark Hall-Patton
"Produced in cooperation with the San Luis Obispo County
    Historical Society."
Bibliography: p.129 Includes index.
ISBN: 0-945092-11-3
1. San Luis Obispo (Calif.)—History. 2. San Luis Obispo (Calif.)—
    Description—Views. 3. San Luis Obispo (Calif.) —Industries.
    I. San Luis Obispo County Historical Society. II. Title.

F869.S396K75 1988   88-25914   979.4′78dc19
                                                CIP
Second Edition, Published 1990 by:
    EZ Nature Books
    Post Office Box 4206
    San Luis Obispo, California 93403
    This book authorized and published under special arrange-
    ment with Windsor Publications, Inc., Chatsworth, California

Windsor Publications, Inc.
Elliot Martin, Chairman of the Board
James L. Fish III, Chief Operating Officer

Contents

The Southern Pacific reached San Miguel on October 18, 1886, and brought prosperity to the town for a few years. This photo was taken around 1888. Courtesy, San Luis Obispo County Historical Museum

Morro Rock was first noted by Cabrillo in 1542, and has been a popular beacon for visitors ever since. Photo by Tim Olson

Acknowledgments

E very written history has its beginning, middle, and end. The end cannot possibly be entirely faithful to real life where the ultimate consequences of any given action might occur several centuries from now. Written history, as Charles A. Beard remarked, is "an act of faith." The writer and his editors must place an arbitrary limit on their text, often imposed by limitations of space.

Looking Backward into the Middle Kingdom is the first extensive history of San Luis Obispo County published since 1939. A whole world of change has occurred since that date, calling for a reexamination of the history of discovery, exploration, and pioneer settlement.

Early on, authors and historians, most especially Clyde Arbuckle of Santa Clara, California, Paul Squibb of Cambria, Ruth Paulding of Arroyo Grande, and Don McMillan of Shandon, pointed to the inadequacies of the existing texts.

Lura Rawson, past director of the San Luis Obispo County Museum, also urged that this project be undertaken as a comprehensive reassessment of the existing literature.

Here, then, is a "new" history, fully recognizing our considerable debt to historic author Myron Angel and his successors.

This volume would not have been possible without the constant support of Mark Hall-Patton, director of the County Historical Museum, who did the photo research and read the text at each stage of development. Mark was ably assisted by Sharon Juhnke and Nora Genthner. No picture history of the Central Coast would be possible without the collection of historic photographs assembled by Irene Carpenter. The San Luis Obispo County Historical Society is truly fortunate as the recipient of the Carpenter collection.

Stan Harth lent his consummate talents to the editing of the original drafts. Stan's sentence-by-sentence editing of the first three chapters was remarkable and saved many weeks of rewriting. Patrick and Eleanor Brown, Lurene F. Milton, and Dudley Parish each read the finished manuscript and made necessary corrections. I alone must take full responsibility for any remaining errors.

Kim Myers Hogan and Susan Wells, manuscript editor and photo director at Windsor Publications, have been helpful throughout the project. Their patience is greatly appreciated.

Tim Olson, photographer for the volume, proved himself an artist in the field with his camera for the "now" views. He is also a wizard of lensmanship in recopying deteriorated ancient photographs for the "then" images.

Finally, both Mark Hall-Patton and I wish to express our gratitude for the love and understanding of our wives, Colleen Hall-Patton and Liz Krieger. They had to endure our many late nights of work, canceled weekend trips, and a multitude of other inconveniences "for the duration."

Dan Krieger
San Luis Obispo, California
July 18, 1988

This wharf served the San Luis Lightstation at Port San Luis. Overland connections to the lighthouse were very rough and most supplies were brought in by ship. Courtesy, San Luis Obispo County Historical Museum

PART ONE

Welcome to the Middle Kingdom

San Luis Obispo County is often referred to as the northernmost of the tri-counties area known as the Central Coast. The Tolkienesque aphorism "Middle Kingdom," first used by Cal Poly students in the early 1970s and later picked up by *National Geographic*, seems more appropriate.

To those who dwell in and love the Middle Kingdom, the quality of life precedes the issue of centrality. Moreover, San Luis Obispo, traditionally the halfway point between San Francisco and Los Angeles, has historically found itself in the "middle" —from the days of early navigators who witnessed the considerable change in weather as they rounded points Conception and Arguello, to the era when San Luis Obispo was the "middle mission," to ranching days when disillusioned Californios like Andres Pico sought to have the southern seven counties severed from the state, with San Luis Obispo as the capital of the "Territory of the Colorado," to modern times when the county received electrical services from Pacific Gas and Electric while natural gas was supplied by Southern California Gas.

Today, the county continues to be in the middle, with allegiances to both Northern and Southern California: the majority of sports fans in the region tend to support the San Francisco 49ers football team but the Los Angeles Dodgers baseball team, and the *San Francisco Chronicle* outsells the *Los Angeles Times*, yet most residents receive cable television service featuring primarily Los Angeles channels.

The region is looked upon as a bellwether for students of both politics and commercial enterprise. If voting patterns are decidedly split in San Luis Obispo County, chances are the remainder of the state of California will be so inclined. Movie makers preview many new films here—often months before they are released elsewhere. Manufacturers try out innovative products in our markets. California Polytechnic State University has become the favorite campus of all 19 of the California State Universities—perhaps in part because it too is "in the middle."

Our history reflects that sense of balance. Young people born and raised here go off elsewhere to receive their educations and find careers, yet return to retire in the Middle Kingdom. It is to those third, fourth, and fifth generation San Luis Obispans, whose memories and consciousness of the importance of history have so enriched the life of our community, that this book is dedicated.

View from the Lake of the Skinny Bear

The Central Coast and San Luis Obispo County have always been a stopping place for travelers. From European mariners who sailed along the jagged coastline, to Franciscan padres, railroad builders, and motorists, the natural topography has obliged all to pause among the scenic wonders of this Middle Kingdom.

Points Conception, Arguello, and Sal form a sea barrier. At the southwestern border of San Luis Obispo County, cool northern waters encounter warmer southern waters. This is the turning point of the California coastline, the site of numerous maritime disasters. On September 8, 1923, at Honda, just north of Point Arguello, the United States Navy's Destroyer Squadron Eleven made a navigational error. This coincided with the tsunami from the great Kanto earthquake in Japan which reversed the currents in the vicinity of Point Conception. Seven of the "four stackers" ran aground in one of the most spectacular disasters in peacetime naval history. *Honda* is a Spanish contraction meaning "deep trail," which suggests the terror that the area held for mariners in the age of sail. Inland from the jagged rocks

The Cuyama Valley in the extreme south of the county was a natural path from the southern San Joaquin Valley to the sea, used by the Native Americans. Today Highway 166 traverses the valley. Photo by Mark P. Hall-Patton

Raphael Solares was one of the last shamans of the Chumash when Leon de Cessic photographed him in 1877. De Cessic's research on the central coast was supposed to be financed by Alphonse Pinart who subsequently did not pay him. De Cessic eventually lived with Pierre H. Dallidet in San Luis Obispo and left his collection with him with the understanding that it would not be given to Pinart. Through the efforts of the French Consulate, the collection was eventually given to the Musee de l'Homme in Paris. Courtesy, Musee de l'Homme

offshore are the Santa Lucia Mountains, a major obstacle for those traveling north by land.

Points Conception, Arguello, and Sal delayed the very first known European explorer along the Central Coast for nearly a month during the autumn of 1542.

Juan Rodriguez Cabrillo sailed into the northern Santa Barbara Channel in mid-October 1542. He was favorably impressed with the Native Americans. The Chumash were members of the Penutian language family, who followed a hunting and gathering lifestyle, both marine and inland, between Point Dume in Malibu and Point Estero north of Cayucos, which got its name in 1769 from the presence of many small fishing boats or canoes.

Cabrillo observed that these prehistoric residents of the Central Coast wore animal skins and tied their hair in cords with tiny daggers of bone, flint, and wood embedded in the braids. They knew about *oep* (maize), but did not raise it. Some of the natives reported that there was oep in the interior hinterlands, along with *cae* (cattle or elk). They sailed great distances in their *pizmo-* or *brea-* (tar) caulked *tomols* (canoes). Cabrillo first encountered the Chumash off Santa Catalina, nearly a hundred miles from their nearest population center. Just off Gaviota, they offered to exchange sardines for the glass trading beads and other gifts that they apparently knew were carried by Spanish

mariners. This suggests that word of Cabrillo's earlier encounters with native Californians farther to the south had reached the Central Coast before the Spanish arrived.

Cabrillo made several attempts to round the wind-swept Point Conception, but ultimately returned to the Goleta area, where he was hosted by the Chumash over the All Saints' Holydays (October 30—November 1, 1542). They fed the Spaniards pinole and acorn mush cakes, which Cabrillo said were very much like tamales "and good to eat." Cabrillo noted that the land south of Point Conception was "more than excellent . . . [a] good country where you can make a settlement."

But settlement was not his mission. Antonia de Mendoza, the viceroy of New Spain, had dispatched him to find treasure that would exceed the Aztec trove captured by Mendoza's archrival and predecessor, Hernando de Cortez. Cabrillo also was ordered to discover the legendary Strait of Anian, or Northwest Passage, fabled to connect the Pacific and Atlantic oceans in northern latitudes. So Cabrillo had to proceed north. On November 11, a southerly gale swept his flotilla around Point Conception, which his men named *Cabo de Galera* because its jutting cliffs resembled a seagoing galley. The storm-tossed seas did not permit safe anchorage along San Luis Obispo County's shores, and the explorer saw little that attracted comment. He ultimately sailed

Left: John Peabody Harrington was the major ethnographer to study the Chumash. His informants were some of the last mission-era Chumash, and his research notes continue to show us the richness of Chumash culture. In this circa-1920 photograph Harrington is shown wearing a Chumash costume. Courtesy, San Luis Obispo County Historical Museum

Right: The Chumash and Salinan Indians of San Luis Obispo used bedrock mortars like these found near Cambria to grind acorns and other seeds for preparing food. Photo by Dr. J. Barron Wiley. Courtesy, San Luis Obispo County Historical Museum

north of Point Reyes, missed San Francisco Bay, and turned back near the mouth of the Russian River.

Returning south, the explorers observed the Santa Cruz Mountains and even snow-covered Cypress Point on the Monterey Peninsula. The weather was so wintry that the seamen could barely cling to the ships' rigging. The climate of the Central California coast was far more moist and cool than it is today. Those same meteorological conditions persisted throughout the Spanish and Mexican periods of occupation, until the early 1860s.

The expedition sighted some settlements along Estero Bay, probably between Cayucos and present-day Morro Bay. High winds and unsettled seas kept the ships far off shore. The condition of the badly leaking *San Miguel* had worsened to the point that the crew thought it was doomed.

The fleet wintered in the Channel Islands, where Cabrillo died on January 3, 1543, probably of a gangrenous infection

from a bone broken in a fall, according to Harry Kelsey in *Juan Rodriguez Cabrillo.*

Recognizing that he was dying, Cabrillo attempted to put his logs in order and complete a report to Viceroy Mendoza, but he did not have sufficient strength to record the details of his voyage north of Point Conception. So our knowledge of San Luis Obispo County in the mid-sixteenth century is fragmentary.

Cabrillo's pilot, Bartolome Ferrer (or Ferrelo), took over command and sailed northward again, scudding before a storm. He sailed as far as the Eel River—and possibly to the Rogue River in Oregon—before scurvy forced him to return to Navidad in New Spain. He arrived on April 14, 1543, with no good news to report about California or the Central Coast.

The Cabrillo expedition tells us much about the limitations imposed by climate and geography on the development of the Central Coast region. The rugged coastline, lack of sheltered anchorages, extended

Top: The Painted Rock of the Carrizo Plains was a Chumash ceremonial site for many years before the Spanish came to this area. During the American Period it became a favorite tourist site, as well as a convenient corral for sheep. The stone wall to fence in the sheep can be seen next to the wagon in this circa-1885 view. Courtesy, San Luis Obispo County Historical Museum

Bottom: Chumash rock art can be found from the Cuesta to Malibu. One of the best known is the Painted Rock of the Carrizo Plains. This photograph taken by R.R.R. Holmes in 1876 is the earliest known of the site. Courtesy, San Luis Obispo County Historical Museum

storm season, and stiff south-bound Japan Current made the area almost inaccessible by sea. Following the Cabrillo expedition, there were no further efforts to visit Central California for four decades.

In 1564 King Philip II ordered a Spanish fleet to find a practicable return route from the Philippine Islands. The Portuguese route via East Africa had been severed by an unprecedented alliance of Islamic pirates. Andres Urdaneta, taking advantage of the Japan Current, established the "Manila galleon" sea route to carry silver bullion and manufactured goods from Mexico to Manila to be traded for spices, silks, and chinaware. These treasures would be carried to Acapulco via the Japan Current from the vicinity of Cape Mendocino. By the 1570s California was acquiring a new importance as a way station in world trade. This would play a major role in shaping the development of the Central Coast during the Mexican and early American periods.

On the four-month-long return voyages from the Philippines, potable water supplies were exhausted. The larder became rancid or filled with maggots. Thousands of crew members died of scurvy. By the early 1580s the viceroy of New Spain, troubled by so calamitous a loss of manpower, had decided that a safe port was needed along the coast of Alta California. The captains of the galleons were ordered to sail close to the rugged coast to search

for a safe harbor and a nearby supply of natural resources.

In 1587 Pedro de Unamuno, a pilot on the Manila galleon route, landed near the mouth of Chorro Creek, near the present site of Morro Bay. Unamuno marched five leagues (12 miles) up either the Los Osos or Chorro valley—"about as far as the present San Luis Obispo," according to a modern authority on Spanish maritime history. Evidently, Unamuno's party fled after several skirmishes with Indians, and Morro Bay lost its first opportunity to become a major seaport. Tree rings and fossilized plants suggest that the San Luis Obispo region would have had sparse vegetation because of the extremely cool climate

that prevailed during this period.

On November 11, 1595, another Spanish mariner made close contact with the San Luis Obispo region. Rodriguez Cermenho had left Manila the preceding July as captain of the galleon *San Agostin.* Following orders from the viceroy, Cermenho made his first landfall just north of Humboldt Bay. He proceeded down the coast, searching for a safe harbor. The *San Agostin* was badly damaged on November 30, when it ran aground during a storm off Cape Mendocino. Cermenho fashioned an open launch, the *San Buenaventura,* from the wreckage and continued his search. As he sailed off Point Buchon, near the present-day nuclear gen-

Seven of the nine peaks which run from San Luis Obispo to Morro Bay are shown in this photograph. The peaks, from Morro Bay inland, are Morro Rock, Black Hill, Cabrillo Peak, Hollister Peak, Cerro Romualdo, Chumash Peak, Bishop's Peak, San Luis Mountain, and Islay Hill. These magma-extrusive mountains have been noted landmarks since Cabrillo's time. Courtesy, San Luis Obispo County Historical Museum

erating facility at Diablo Canyon, his crew sighted many Chumash on the rocky cliffs. The Spaniards heard the natives cry "Christinos" and "Mexico" —words probably acquired during the visit of Unamuno eight years earlier.

While Manila galleons continued to ply the coastal waters off San Luis Obispo, the next important contact did not occur until 1602-1603, when Sebastian Vizcaino sailed up from Mexico with two small ships and a launch. Vizcaino had promised the viceroy of New Spain, the Marquis de Monterey, that he would locate a good harbor for the Manila galleons. It was he who "discovered" Monterey Bay, though it had been previously noted by Cabrillo, Unamuno, and Cermenho. He exaggerated its qualities as a harbor and had his cartographer draw a distorted map depicting a fully enclosed bay. This caused great confusion in the subsequent exploration of California by land. He also renamed many of the sites observed by earlier navigators, including the Santa Lucia Mountains, which became a landmark for locating proximity to his "magnificent harbor." Historians believe that Vizcaino probably entered San Luis Bay and traded with the Chumash.

The Marques de Montesclaros, the next viceroy, was unconvinced by Vizcaino's reports and maps of a great harbor at Monterey. Royal officials believed further voyages to California or attempted landings by the Manila galleons were not worth the risk. Thus, Vizcaino apparently was the last European to make contact with the California coast or San Luis Obispo for 167 years.

In 1765 King Charles III appointed Jose de Galvez, an enthusiastic expansionist, as *visitador general,* or inspector general to New Spain. In this position, ranking above even the viceroy, Galvez nebulously assumed that the Russians, in their expansion east through Siberia, might pose a threat to California.

Galvez's rise to power coincided with Spain's expelling the powerful religious order known as the Society of Jesus, or Jesuits, from throughout its empire. The Jesuits had established a chain of missions in the southern half of Baja California. These so-called "Black Robes" were to be replaced with the "Gray Friars," or Franciscans. Thus, Galvez was brought into contact with Father Junipero Serra and his band of energetic priests, as well as with the soldier-explorer Gaspar de Portola.

Serra, Portola, Father Juan Crespi, and the majority of soldiers and Franciscan priests sent to colonize Alta California came from Catalonia, in southeastern Spain. In terms of topography and climate, Catalonia resembles California. The men of the so-called "Sacred Expedition" knew how to deal with the terrain and climate.

Galvez directed that expedition's leader, Portola, to sail to the southern Baja California seaport of La Paz. From there, Portola, along with fathers Serra and Crespi, were to proceed up the peninsula overland to San Diego to meet with three ships, the San Carlos, the San Antonio, and the San Jose. They were then to march north in search of Vizcaino's Monterey Bay. The ships also were to sail north; presumably both the land and sea branches of the enterprise would rendezvous in the great harbor. Unfortunately the San Jose was lost at sea with all hands. The San Carlos and the San Antonio lost nearly half of their crews to scurvy and were in no condition to sail farther north. Nor was Serra able to proceed beyond San Diego. Crespi, the expedition's diarist, reported that an ulcerated abscess on Serra's leg, the result of a snake or insect bite, had impaired the father-presidente's ability to travel. So the search for Monterey Bay was left to Captain Portola, Father Crespi, and a party of 63 soldiers and Indian porters. They left San Diego on July 14, 1769, blazing a trail which, for the most part, became El Camino Real, California's trail of 19 missions between San Diego and San Francisco.

Father Crespi proved to be an excellent observer, writing in his diary about what he witnessed in the late summer and autumn of 1769 as he traveled with the first overland journey made by European explorers.

The column of men, plus just under 200 horses and pack animals, was about a half-mile long, traveling single file on the narrow trail. At its head were two or three Catalonian volunteers wearing heavy, multi-layered, apron-like leather jackets, their armor against stone-pointed projectiles, wildcats, and bears, the chief hazards they anticipated. In the hot, dry climate of the Sonoran Desert and the chaparral of Baja and Alta California, they wore felt or straw sombreros rather than their usual plumed leather helmets.

Carrying shields of tough bull's hide, the enlisted men rode sure-footed mules that were so overladen with gear that only the long ears and "donkey's tails" revealed their species. The soldiers carried both sheathed machetes and sabers in scabbards. A long leather holster was fixed to each mule's back. This contained a Seven Years' War-era musket—a smooth-bore firearm without sights, designed for firing from a massed infantry formation in the hope that one of the many balls might strike the target. The musket had a short range, and while it could easily kill thin-skinned creatures like man, it often required half a dozen hits to bring down a bear or other large animal. Its chief advantage was its noise and the flame and smoke it created; the audio-visual effects had a considerable power of intimidation over Native Americans.

Next in the column came 10 or 12 nearly naked Indian scouts drawn from the mission-ized tribes of Baja California. They each carried a machete or an ax, an iron or oak pry bar, and a shovel or mattock for clear-ing the trail.

Portola came next, followed by Ensign Miguel de Costanso, Lieutenant Pedro Fages, and six more Catalonian volunteers.

Then came the two gray-robed Franciscan friars, Juan Crespi and Francisco Gomez. Each wore gray or brown felt "barber's shaving pan" hats, which resembled overdone poached eggs. The padres rode mules and were unarmed. They carried blanket rolls, glass beads as gifts for the Indians, and writing materials, plus a compass, astrolabe, and quadrant for ascertaining latitude.

More than 100 mules came next. One or two mounted mule skinners accompanied each section of 25 mules. They were followed by several dozen unsaddled horses and mules, many of them sick or limping. At the rear of the column was Captain Fernando de Rivera y Moncada.

The expedition tried to stay in sight of the Pacific Ocean, but it had to travel inland at San Juan Capistrano and Ventura to avoid marshy estuaries filled with brackish water. On Monday, August 28, the party passed Point Arguello and camped near Honda. The soldiers wandered out onto a jagged strip of land which extended into the sea. According to the diary kept by Lieutenant Miguel de Costanso (formerly ensign), the engineer for the expedition, "We gathered a great deal of flint stones for our firearms, and consequently the spot was called los Pedernales, the Flints."

On August 30 they crossed the Santa Maria River and

were in what is now San Luis Obispo County. They had not eaten meat for several days. On Saturday, September 2, they observed numerous bear tracks and succeeded in shooting a tall, scrawny bear next to a lake. Costanso called this "Round Lake," but Father Crespi reported that others in the expedition called it El Oso Flaco—The Skinny Bear. Today motorists can visit Oso Flaco Lake much as it was in 1769. From atop the adjoining dunes, the Santa Lucia Range is clearly visible across the open sea. The lake is west of Highway 1 and three miles north of Guadalupe.

The bear evidently had consumed an alkaloid poison, perhaps intentionally put in meat by natives. The alkaloid would numb the bear's legs, making it easier for the Chumash to kill with their primitive weapons. The morning after consuming the bear meat—which was "well flavored and good"—the men had difficulty standing. The first Central Coast barbecue consumed by Europeans had been poisonous!

Moving north through the Nipomo Mesa and on to Arroyo Grande Creek, they encountered a prosperous village governed by a powerful chieftain whom the soldiers nicknamed "El Buchon" because of his enormous goiter. Later, Chief Buchon would be instrumental in assisting the missionary settlement at San Luis Obispo.

The expedition turned inland onto the bluffs above Grover City and Pismo Beach,

Facing page: This circa-1885 photo shows Morro Rock before extensive quarrying had begun. Morro Rock was noted by Cabrillo in his exploration of the California coast in 1542. In 1587 Pedro de Unamuno became the first European to visit the county, coming ashore at Morro Bay and exploring inland to approximately where the city of San Luis Obispo is today. Courtesy, San Luis Obispo County Historical Museum

then crossed the Ontario Grade into the Irish Hills above the Los Osos Valley on September 5-7, 1769. The southern mouth of the valley was filled with a series of miry-shored lagoons. This is the present Laguna Lake area. The men headed northwest along the foothills for three miles, then camped not far from the present intersection of Los Osos Valley and Turri roads. It had been five days since they had eaten fresh meat. Here Crespi notes:

We saw troops of bears which kept the ground plowed up and full of holes which they made searching for roots which constitute their food, and on which the heathen [Native Americans] also live . . . The soldiers went out to hunt and succeeded in killing one with bullets, in doing which they learned the ferocity of these animals. When they feel themselves wounded they attack the hunter at full speed, and he can escape only by the dexterity of his horse. They do not yield until they [the soldiers] get a shot at the head or the heart. This one that they killed received nine balls before he fell, which did not happen until one struck him in the head. Some of the soldiers were fearless enough to chase one of these animals mounted on poor beasts. They fired seven or eight shots, and I have no doubt he would die from the balls; but the bear upset two of the mules, and it was only by good fortune that the two mounted on them escaped with their lives. This valley they named Los Osos [the bears], and I called it La Natividad de Nuestra Senora [the birth of Our Lady].

The explorers would remember this "Bear Hollow" or *La Canada de Los Osos* as an abundant source of meat.

The expedition left there the next day and headed north along the current South Bay Boulevard, camping near the present-day Los Osos Junior High School. Costanso observed a "small-sized . . . village . . . amounting to sixty souls . . . They [the natives] offered us a sort of gruel made out of parched seeds which we all thought tasted well, with a flavor of almonds."

The explorers also saw Morro Bay for the first time:

Upon the south side, there reaches up into this hollow an inlet of enormous size, which we thought must be a harbor; however, its mouth, which opens up southwestward, is covered by reefs that give rise to a raging surf. A short distance northward of the mouth . . . was seen an extremely large rock shaped like a round head [morro, from a Moor's turban], which at high tide, becomes an island separated from the shore . . . Beyond this head the coast trends westnorthwestward as far as a big point [Point Estero].

Portola's men traced the eventual route of Highway 1 past Point Estero, camping on Sunday, September 10, near the current Coast Union High School of Cambria, along the bank of Santa Rosa Creek. On the 11th they camped at the mouth of Pico Creek. The next day, the march became more rugged, over thickly grown knolls. On

the 13th they realized they must be at the base of the Santa Lucia Range, which they had first seen from the dunes above Oso Flaco Lake.

On the 14th Portola's scouts confirmed that mountains blocked their further passage north. The next day, the scouts worked with pry bars, pick axes, and machetes to prepare a path up Carpoforo Creek. On the 16th they made the steep ascent, crossing the crest of the Santa Lucia Range into what is now Monterey County. On Saturday, September 23, they sighted the Salinas River, which they took to be the Carmelo River. According to Vizcaino's deceptive map, this would lead them just south of Monterey Bay. The rest of the story counts among the more noteworthy episodes in California history: How Portola's men failed to recognize Monterey Bay when they reached the Pacific at the mouth of the Salinas River, assuming that the "great harbor" was farther to the north. They proceeded north, even though their calculations indicated that they had passed the 37th parallel.

On November 11 the expedition turned south and, retracing their earlier march upcountry, reentered what is now San Luis Obispo County on December 20. They spent Christmas at Cambria. It was a meatless feast but as Father Crespi records, near Cayucos they came "close to a small village of Indian fishermen, from whom a great deal of fish was obtained, in exchange for beads . . . So we celebrated Christmas with this dainty, which tasted better to everybody than capons and chickens . . . because of the good sauce of San Bernardo, [meaning] hunger." Saint Francis had termed fasting "the feast of San Bernardo" after Saint Bernard of Clairvaux, the twelfth-century monastic reformer whose Cistercian Order of monks emphasized, among other sacrifices, fasting.

The only alteration the party made in retracing its steps was to exit from the Los Osos Valley by way of the Edna Valley so that "we would come out at the *Plan de los Berros* [Watercress Flat along the southern bank of Arroyo Grande Creek] or Buchon's Village." Again, Chief Buchon supplied the explorers with "a plentiful present of gruel, mush and very good-sized tamales that looked as if made from corn."

On the whole, though the expedition had been impeded by the rugged Santa Lucia Mountains, the San Luis Obispo County region had been quite good to the first Europeans to explore this land.

Saints, Padres, and Ordinary People

I n 1770 Portola made a second overland journey in search of Monterey Bay, and it was, indeed, Vizcaino's harbor. The ship *San Antonio* arrived a week after Portola, and on June 3, 1770, Father Serra said mass beneath the same oak under which Vizcaino had celebrated mass in 1602. A presidio was established, and Mission San Carlos de Barromeo was founded.

The missions served a dual purpose. First, from the standpoint of imperial Spain, the missions were a low-cost way of colonizing frontier lands. With just a handful of missionaries and soldiers, thousands of native inhabitants could be converted to Christianity and made loyal citizens of Spain. A Franciscan mission was intended to become, within one or two decades, a self-sufficient Hispanic pueblo, very much like the villages of Mexico. The Franciscans then could be reassigned to fresh frontier fields. Second, the church would benefit by converting the mission edifice to a parish, staffed by parish priests, under the supervision of a bishop.

When fathers Serra, Palou, Crespi, and the other Franciscans accepted the assignment to California in 1767-1768,

Founded by Father Lasuen in 1797, Mission San Miguel served the Salinan Indians of the northern San Luis Obispo County area. Very prosperous, it boasted a population of 5,000 in its heyday, and controlled ranchos stretching to the coast and south to Paso Robles. Courtesy, R. Dana Holt

they were perfectly willing to endure the hardships of this remote outpost. The task offered the opportunity of doing the Lord's work in a place where the gospel had never been preached—of converting the native Californians into "God's own children," so named for their innocence and trust. Unfortunately, though talented and energetic builders, the missionaries had a typically premodern belief in the superiority of their own culture, viewing the native Californians as a hopelessly backward people who had to be protected from secular influences. It was in their desire to shield the neophytes ("newly planted seeds," the Franciscans' term for all the Indian converts, no matter how long they had been Christianized) from "contamination" by outside influences that the padres came into conflict with the Spanish military governors.

On July 9, 1770, Portola sailed from Monterey aboard the *San Antonio*. He had pressing family business in Spain and never returned to California. He turned his command as military governor of the province of Alta California over to Lieutenant Pedro Fages. Fages had been in command of the Catalonian soldiers hunting grizzly bears in the Los Osos Valley during the first Portola expedition the previous September.

Serra and Fages began to quarrel, initially over Serra's plan to found new missions. Fages contended that he did not have sufficient manpower and material resources to staff them.

The new governor was cor-

rect. He had only 19 soldiers at Monterey and 22 at San Diego under Captain Fernando de Rivera y Moncada. There were only four priests. Serra was just beginning to recover from a serious bout with scurvy. In an incident at San Diego, Father Jose Vizcaino had been shot with an arrow and was still suffering from the wound. At one point in January and February 1770, Portola himself had been prepared to abandon Alta California.

But Serra was a man of fierce determination. He regarded Fages as an obstruction to "God's work." So the quarrel expanded to virtually every aspect of military-missionary relations. The arrival of 10 priests aboard the *San Antonio* on May 21, 1771, gave Serra the opportunity to found a mission in the *Hoya de la Sierra de Santa Lucia,* which he called *Canada de los Robles* (The Valley of the Oaks). Here, amid a magnificent stand of oaks first observed by the Portola expedition, Serra established Mission San Antonio de Padua.

He also moved San Carlos Mission from the presidio site in Monterey to the lower Carmelo River Valley. Ostensibly this was to find more fertile land and supplies of water, but Serra also wished to remove his precious neophytes from the corrupting influence of the soldiers at the presidio.

A fourth mission was founded in the eastern Los Angeles basin, along the banks of the Rio de San Gabriel. Serra wanted to situate a fifth mis-

sion at San Buenaventura in November 1771. Fages refused, declaring that progress at the existing missions was too slow. Serra and Palou countered that this was due to the interference of the soldiers, some of whom lassoed native women at several of the *rancherias* (Indian encampments) to fulfill their lust and killed males who dared to interfere.

During the spring of 1772 all four missions experienced near-starvation conditions. Late in May Fages led an expedition of 13 men to La Canada de Los Osos to hunt grizzly bears. Fages and his men spent three months in the Los Osos Valley and dispatched 25 loads (about 9,000 pounds) of salted bear meat and air-dried jerky to missions San Antonio and San Carlos.

The assured supply of food in the region evidently caused Serra to switch his immediate goal from the founding of a mission at San Buenaventura to the creation of a missionary base in La Canada de Los Osos. Serra justified the change, at least partially, on reports that Fages' hunters had committed numerous illicit acts with the native women in the Los Osos area. Fages was about to leave for San Diego, so Serra decided to accompany him, hoping to establish a mission in the Valley of the Bears with Fages' approval. He expected to assign both fathers Jose Caveller and Domingo Juncosa to the new enterprise, but Father Domingo was needed to take the place of an ailing Francis-

can at Mission Carmelo.

Captain Fages apparently approved of Serra's plan, for in mid-August 1772, a "mule train . . . bearing the supplies, the vestments and other church goods" for the founding of the new mission departed from the presidio in Monterey.

How then did the mission come to be founded in San Luis Obispo rather than the Los Osos Valley? Father Francisco Palou's contemporary account explains:

[By the] time the company arrived in the vicinity of Bear Valley [and] after surveying the locality, it was determined to found the Mission about half a league [1.25 miles] before reaching the Canada de los Osos, yet in sight of it, on a level plot which appeared to be most suitable for the Mission on account of two little arroyos which contained water with sufficient lands that with little trouble . . . could be irrigated from them.

A number of Chumash, who were then residing in the Los Osos Valley and the lower reaches of San Luis Obispo Creek, watched with interest as the mission was founded. Serra inscribed the frontal page of the *Registro de Bautismos* (the Baptismal Register) that the mission was "begun on the first day of September of the year 1772. On that day, the undersigned, President of these missions, with the assistance of Father . . . Joseph Caveller, blessed the site, set up the Holy Cross and sang the first Mass." The mass was probably preceded by a vigorous ringing of a bell to summon potential converts. If the usual practice was followed, the mass was celebrated in a quickly constructed *enramada* (shelter) of tules and brush palisades. The mass would have been followed by the soldiers' firing a volley from their muskets and a small cannon—both in observance of the portentous event and to demonstrate the Spaniards' superiority of armaments.

The next day Serra and Fages left for San Diego.

Carlton E. Watkins, one of California's premier photographers of the nineteenth century, took this shot of Mission San Luis Obispo before it was sided with wood in 1883. One of the new gaslights in town is shown near the site of the 1858 Committee of Vigilance gallows. Courtesy, San Luis Obispo County Historical Museum

Left: Mission San Luis Obispo's gristmill on San Luis Creek ran with a waterwheel and was the second gristmill for the mission. It stood until the early 1970s, when it was being used as a guesthouse. Courtesy, San Luis Obispo County Historical Museum

Right: In its heyday, Mission San Luis Obispo supported a population of nearly 1,000. This is a fragment of the wall of one of the outbuildings of the mission. The wall stands behind the present County Historical Museum. This view from about 1890 shows the home of Ramona Pacheco Wilson and Captain John Wilson which burned in 1898. Many of the children in San Luis Obispo were sheltered in this home during the vigilante actions of June 1858. Courtesy, San Luis Obispo County Historical Museum

Caveller was left to get the mission going on his own. It was a solitary role that he would have to play during his remaining 17 years.

Serra left Caveller with five soldiers, under the command of Corporal Vincente Briones, and two missionized Indians from Baja California. The latter were not particularly effective interpreters, since their language stemmed from that of the Uto-Aztecan family and the Chumash spoke a Hokan dialect.

Caveller's material resources also were meager. Francisco Palou, in his *Life of Serra,* lists the supplies for the new mission: "fifty pounds of flour, three pecks [three-fourths of a bushel] of wheat for sowing, a quantity of chocolate [in the form of small balls for making beverages], and a box of brown sugar for which they might obtain wild seeds from the gentiles."

Caveller was both energetic and enterprising, using his meager provisions to full advan-

tage. He wrote, in his report to Father Palou in Baja California, that

as soon as [Serra and Fages] had set out on their journey . . . [I had] the two Indians . . . cut wood [and] construct a small chapel which might also serve as a shelter . . . At the same time the soldiers made their own quarters, and constructed a stockade for their defense.

Caveller soon discovered that the mission had been located some distance from the nearest Indian settlement. In attempting to instruct the Chumash in the Christian religion, he suffered a setback when two parents permitted him to baptize their son, who was dying. The boy died soon after receiving the waters of baptism. There were no candidates for the rite of conversion for many months.

There is an ironic twist to the story of the fledgling mission's survival during this period of short supplies. Serra had originally contended that the mission in the Canada de Los Osos was necessary to repair the damage done by the misconduct of the soldiers who hunted there during the summer of 1772. Yet, Caveller said when the Indians encountered soldiers who had been on that bear hunt among the new mission's *escolte* (guard) they

gratefully thanked them for having rid their country of so many fierce animals which had killed so many Indians, of those who were yet alive not a few bore the marks of those terrible bear claws. They therefore expressed themselves as very well satisfied that we had made our home in their country. They frequently visited the mission, bringing . . . presents of venison and wild seeds, and getting in exchange beads and brown sugar. By means of this assistance from the wild [unconverted] Indians the Christians were enabled to maintain themselves until the arrival of the ship which brought their provisions.

By the end of the year, 12 children from four families had been converted. And by 1784, the year of Serra's death, Palou had recorded 616 baptisms at the mission.

In 1774 a new and more permanent church was erected, measuring 24 by 60 feet. It had adobe foundations, but its superstructure was made of shaved limbs and tules.

On the night of November 29, 1776, a disastrous fire destroyed nearly the entire mission. Palou summarized the reports of this fire:

At about one o'clock, the sentinel saw a great fire back of the dwelling of the Fathers. It seemed that the kitchen was burning. He notified the corporal, who immediately with the rest of the soldiers aroused from their sleep hastened to the mission which already was afire.

The soldiers found all of the neophytes asleep in the rancheria. They presumed that the fire had to have been set by outsiders.

The loss to the mission was disastrous. The priests' quarters, all the furniture and farm implements, and the granary were destroyed. The soldiers feared that a general Indian uprising was under way. The military governor at Monterey was summoned. Captain Fernando Rivera y Moncada, who had been exploring the Sacramento-San Joaquin River Delta, ordered a forced march to San Luis Obispo. Once there, his investigations revealed that the fires had indeed been deliberately set. A group of Indians some 25 miles from the Mission was held responsible. Palou suggested that the arson was an act of pure frustration by Indians, who were powerless to attack their traditional enemies and who decided to set fire to the mission's tule roofs.

Modern historians have perceived a more rational reason for the attack. Non-missionized Chumash from the Cuyama Valley, or possibly Yokuts from the San Joaquin Valley, may have set the fires as a distraction while they stole horses from the corral. Prior to the Indus-

trial Age, the Native American feared the horse more than any other of the white man's technologies, including firearms.

The raid and fire were only temporary setbacks. No doubt Caveller was embarrassed when he reported that celebrating mass was impossible on the following day because all of the altar wine and beeswax candles had been destroyed in the fire. But the highly strategic location of the mission and its excellent economic potential assured the permanence of the Hispanic settlement.

The mission had been located in the region because of the availability of the much needed bear meat, although most of the grizzly bears were eliminated in Fages' hunting expedition prior to the mission's founding. Palou writes of the gratitude of the local Chumash, "because their territory had been delivered from those fierce animals, which had killed many Indians." The fertile, well-irrigated lands at the southern base of the Santa Lucia Range promised agricultural prosperity that was soon realized. Moreover, Mission San Luis Obispo was located at the center of the El Camino Real, the public highway connecting the mission chain. All travelers up and down the highway gladly stopped at the pleasant mission.

Palou, in his report to the viceroy, *Informe,* dated December 10, 1773, emphasized the centrality of San Luis Obispo, which rested almost equidistant between the Santa Barbara Chan-

27

nel and Mission San Antonio de Padua. Then, in March 1776, Juan Bautista de Anza, bringing 200 settlers overland from the Valley of Mexico, took a route north from San Luis Obispo quite different from the path taken by Portola in 1769. Anza went up Cuesta Canyon, just west of the present-day freeway. Caveller and his cohorts at San Luis Obispo had discovered the pass through the Santa Lucias to Santa Margarita. The journey north had thus become much shorter and less formidable. In a very real sense, the Anza Trail was crucial to San Luis Obispo's future role as a transportation hub in the age of railroads—and later, in the era of the truck and automobile.

Serra spent very little time in San Luis Obispo. The venerable father-presidente was only briefly present at the time of the mission's founding on September 1, 1772. He returned again on April 30, 1774, en route to Monterey and his beloved Mission Carmelo after six months of conferences with Viceroy Antonio Maria Bucareli y Ursua in the city of Mexico. Although worn by a terrible fever contracted in Mexico, Serra had a successful trip. The viceroy had assured him of an improved schedule of supply

This circa-1910 postcard view shows the old Cuesta road on the left, and the Padre's Trail at the bottom of the pass. The current road was not built until 1915. It received major revisions in 1937. Courtesy, San Luis Obispo County Historical Museum

ships to Alta California and had issued the *Reglamento*, the first set of laws for the new province.

While in Mexico, Serra commissioned oil paintings of the titular saints for the California missions that did not have pictures to adorn their altars. The picture of Saint Louis, Bishop of Toulouse, the thirteenth century figure who became the patron saint of San Luis Obispo de Tolosa, is now known to be an earlier work, probably painted in Spain or Peru. The painting had preceded Serra's arrival at the mission. The father-presidente was tactful in bringing to the attention of Father Caveller the fact that the painting had cost 18 pesos. This amount would be charged against San Luis Obispo's share of the Pious Fund, an account established to aid missions in Baja and Alta California. Caveller would rather have spent the 18 pesos on much needed supplies for his mission. Eighteen pesos was a large sum and would have purchased several badly needed iron plowshares and other farming implements.

Caveller delicately informed Serra that his mission already had a portrait of Saint Louis. Serra replied that the one he had sent was nicer. Caveller suggested that the padres at San Antonio de Padua might like the portrait. The parcel containing the picture was never unwrapped. Serra dropped the matter, and took the portrait with him to Carmelo, transferring the debt to his own mission's account.

There is an oral tradition in San Luis Obispo, unsubstantiated in Palou's *Life of Serra,* that the father-presidente ordered Caveller and Juncosa to accept, pray to, and pay for the painting—asserting that the painting was more important than the material things of life. That same painting now hangs in the 1948 annex to the mission church in San Luis Obispo. It was evidently returned to the mission from a nearly ruined portion of San Miguel Mission during the pastorate of Father Appollinarius Rouselle, who served at San Luis Obispo from 1874 to 1891.

Serra visited San Luis Obispo again, probably at Christmas 1776. He had spent a storm-swept December traveling through the Chumash rancherias of Ventura and Santa Barbara counties. He described how the *Canalinos* (Chumash of the Channel Islands) sang along with him on his march north. He planned the locations of three missions at Ventura, Santa Barbara, and Point Conception.

While at San Luis Obispo, Serra inspected the damage from the recent fire and convinced a reluctant Father Fermin de Lasuen, the man who was to succeed him as father-presidente, to accept reassignment.

Here we can witness the very human side of the devout Father Serra. He recognized great talent in Lasuen, and thought it probable that the slightly younger priest would succeed him as administrator of the California missions. But relations between the two men had not been easy. Lasuen was a personal friend and admirer of Captain Fernando Rivera y Moncada, the military governor of Alta California. Rivera wanted Lasuen to serve as his personal chaplain at the Presidio of Monterey. Lasuen evidently had no knowledge of the deep divisions between Serra and the governor. Serra opposed the military chaplaincy because no provision had been made for such a post, and priests were sorely needed in the missionary fields of California.

Lasuen was assigned to Mission San Gabriel when he first arrived in Alta California in 1773. His first two years in the remote province evidently were miserable. He wrote repeated requests that he be returned to the city of Mexico. Rivera threatened to resign if Lasuen was not appointed as his chaplain. Serra capitulated, and the *Collegio de San Fernando* (Franciscan administration in Mexico) ultimately granted permission for the appointment.

Then, shortly after Christmas 1776, Serra and Lasuen met at the ruins of the burned-out mission at San Luis Obispo. Serra probably explained matters to Lasuen. Lasuen's attitude toward the chaplaincy immediately changed. He accepted temporary reassignment, helping to rebuild the ruined mission near the Valley of the Bears, serving from January 8 to March 7, 1777. Thereafter he again was reassigned, to take charge of the reconstruction of San Diego Mission follow-

ing a Native American uprising at that mission during which Father Luis Jayme was murdered. Lasuen remained at San Diego until the Collegio de San Fernando appointed him father-presidente on February 6, 1785. Thus San Luis Obispo, as a central meeting point, was the site of events that formed the future years of Spain's remote missionary outpost.

Mission San Luis Obispo suffered two more major fires during its early years, following the disaster of November 29, 1776. A second fire occurred on Christmas Day, 1781, when, according to Caveller, a neophyte from Baja California carelessly discharged a firearm in the midst of the celebration—possibly at the Gloria of the Midnight Mass. Fortunately the congregation provided ample volunteer fire fighters, and damage was kept to a minimum. A third fire occurred in November 1782. Such fires were a common

scourge of the first California missions with their tule roofs.

Palou's writings are regarded among the most reliable primary sources for documenting early mission life. Yet a misunderstanding of Palou's account of the fires at San Luis Obispo has contributed to the creation of a myth. Palou seemed to suggest that fired-clay roof tiles were first used at San Luis Obispo. This, in turn, gave credence to local folklore claiming that Chumash maidens molded the clay on their thighs—a most immodest method, considering the concerns of the Franciscan padres over possible illicit acts between the female neophytes and the mission *escolte,* or soldier-guards.

In fact a letter by Serra, dated December 8, 1781, clearly indicates that tiles were first employed at Mission San Antonio. Moreover the tiles were made using wooden molds, according to a technique as old as Mediterranean culture. Clay tiles were not used at first because their production requires both skill and patience. Once deemed necessary, they were employed at all of the principal mission sites during and after the early 1780s.

Caveller began the construction of San Luis Obispo's present mission church in 1788. He did not live to see it completed. His death on December 9, 1789, coincided with the beginning of an era of prosperity at the mission.

During Caveller's 17 years of administration, 877 baptisms had taken place at the mission. Since 1776 there had been regular agricultural surpluses above what the mission needed to maintain itself. This was, in large part, testimony to the fertile lands in the coastal valleys. The neophyte population stood at 578. Also, the mission was sufficiently prosperous to make an indirect contribution toward the costs incurred by the Bourbon King of Spain in fighting England during the American colonies' War of Independence. In 1782 assessments of approximately $1,000 (in 1988 valuation) were levied against each of the California missions. The payment seems insignificant today, except that it had to be in cash. Not all of the missions were affluent enough to meet this levy. To this extent, San Luis Obispo played a tiny part in the success of the 13 British colonies in winning their independence.

Life at San Luis Obispo was never easy for Caveller. The mission records indicate that he was seldom able to leave San Luis Obispo, and that his handwriting was quite feeble during the last several years of his life. He was only 45 years of age at the time of his death.

Despite his relatively early death, Caveller outlived the vast majority of the Chumash whom he had converted to Christianity. In 1804 the mission population reached its peak at 832. There had been 2,074 baptisms and 1,091 deaths registered in the baptismal and burial records since 1772. Only San Carlos de Borremeo had a smaller number of neophytes. Death and funerals were a common occurrence at the mission.

The high death rate was in large measure due to the Native Americans' lack of immunity to common European diseases. Native Californians, like the peoples of the Pacific Islands, had been cut off from the mainstream of humanity since the end of the Pleistocene epoch. Mumps, measles, chicken pox, boils, the common cold—all could produce massive assaults on the body's defenses, resulting in irreversible pneumonia and death. Smallpox, which had produced deadly epidemics among the Toltec and Aztec peoples around the time of Cortez, reappeared in Southern Mexico in 1797. It took more than 20 years for the disease to migrate north to Alta California. During the period of Mexican rule, smallpox took a great number of lives. Syphilis was both the deadliest and the most insidious killer. The Spanish soldiers of the *escolte* (mission guard) in-

fected hundreds of female neophytes during the early mission period, and the ravages of the disease were passed on to later generations, as evinced from clinical examinations of bones from mission cemeteries.

The number of neophytes in San Luis Obispo peaked in 1804 and began to decline rapidly thereafter. Yet it was during this period that the mission, and its more recent sister mission to the north, San Miguel Archangel, began an era of territorial expansion.

Ironically, the lack of water resources may have triggered this move. In 1790 Governor Pedro Fages wrote that water supplies had become a major problem at San Luis Obispo. The growing population and increasing head of cattle clearly had overtaxed the water supply. Resources had to be allocated over a wide geographical area.

At an unknown date during the 1790s, an auxiliary rancho was established just north of the Cuesta, the steep "hog back" pass over the Santa Lucia Range. The assistant mission was located at a site named for Santa Margarita de Cortona, a thirteenth-century Italian saint. The area was comprised of 17,735 acres of dark, loamy soil by the streams, plus high amounts of clay on the uplands with some adobe, and had a significantly higher rainfall than that of San Luis Obispo. Current rainfall averages for San Luis Obispo and Santa Margarita are 22.32 and 28.41 inches per year, respec-

Mission San Miguel was photographed here in the late 1800s. This view shows some of the last mission Indians near the ruins of the mission quadrangle. Courtesy, Mission San Miguel

tively. Eventually a stone-and-adobe granary and chapel were constructed at the site.

In 1808 and 1809 another granary and chapel, called the Rancho San Miguelito, were constructed at the mouth of San Luis Obispo Creek, near the present-day town of Avila Beach. Later, a small house was built on a site named Arroyo Grande.

In 1797 Mission San Miguel Archangel was founded in the northernmost part of San Luis Obispo County, about 40 miles south of Mission San Antonio and 40 miles north of San Luis Obispo. This was the 16th in the chain of missions. Although the land surrounding it generally was inferior to the lands belonging to San Luis Obispo, the mission prospered through its herds of cattle and horses. Governor Fages had suggested that the missions of this middle land specialize in animal breeding, and it was in this area

that the mission ranchers excelled. San Luis Obispo de Tolosa and San Miguel Archangel, with their outlying ranchos, became the envy of all the other missions when it came to the size and quality of their herds.

The mission enterprises had thrived under Spain's policy of protectionism and benevolent neglect. But the number of neophytes was declining rapidly after the early years of the nineteenth century. The Napoleonic Wars had triggered events that would lead to the independence of Mexico, and after 1822 the covetous eyes of thousands of landless Mexicans would be cast upon the missions with their herds of hardy stock. The mission system was doomed through its own productive successes in terms of crops and animals, along with its failure to build large communities of indigenous peoples.

A sketch by Edward
Vischer shows Mission
San Miguel in 1864. Cour-
tesy, Bancroft Library

Americanization of the Barrio of the Tiger

The California vaquero was noted by travelers in the early-nineteenth century as being the finest horseman in the world. This 1870 sketch by W.H. Hilton shows vaqueros at a rodeo, rounding up the various rancheros' cattle to brand. Courtesy, Bancroft Library

The growth and prosperity of missions San Luis Obispo and San Miguel brought most of the coastal valleys of San Luis Obispo County into the missionaries' sphere of influence. After circa 1800, in the southern portion of the county, patrols from Mission Purisima in the lower Santa Ynez Valley would travel north to the Santa Maria River, where they would exchange pennants with a patrol sent south from San Luis Obispo. It was during the missionary epoch that the border was delineated between San Luis Obispo and Santa Barbara counties.

The lands controlled by the missions were divided into dozens of ranchos, some as much as 40 or 50 thousand acres in size. These ranchos were entrusted to an overseer, residing at a *vista*—usually a sizable adobe structure designed to accommodate travelers as well as the padres on their occasional visits. The Franciscan padres, for all their otherworldliness, had become empire builders in California real estate. Father Juan Vincente Cabot was a prime example of such a builder.

Cabot, born in Catalonia like Serra, was a leader

among the third generation of Spanish Franciscans in California. His first assignment was at Purisima. Later he served at San Miguel, Soledad, San Francisco, and San Miguel again, from 1824 to the time of secularization in 1834.

A circa-1930 photograph shows the adobe home of Pedro Estrada on Rancho Asuncion, the southernmost rancho of Mission San Miguel. Pedro Estrada was granted the rancho in 1845. Estrada's cousin Joaquin Estrada was granted the Santa Margarita Rancho, which, along with Rancho Asuncion and Rancho Atascadero, was acquired by Martin Murphy in the 1860s. After Murphy acquired ownership, the Atascadero and Asuncion ranchos were combined. Courtesy, Southwest Museum, Guy Giffen Collection

He made many military expeditions into the San Joaquin Valley, going as far as the site of the present-day town of Visalia. He urged that Father-Presidente Vincente Francisco de Sarria authorize the establishment of a second chain of missions in the vicinity of the San Joaquin and Kings rivers. Though no mission was ever founded in the valley, on these trips Cabot baptized dozens of *Tularenos,* as the residents of the southern San Joaquin Valley were known, and a significant number of the valley natives at Mission San Miguel. Many historians argue that these treks were intended to capture and punish runaway neophytes, or

else to replenish the dwindling labor force at the missions with virtually enslaved Tularenos. Franciscan historians and their supporters contend that Cabot was merely carrying out the apostolic mandate of bringing the faith to the pagan lands.

Cabot, who may himself have suffered from rheumatism, also constructed a shelter house and a place for bathing over the sulphur springs at Paso Robles. Many of the other mission friars prohibited bathing because of its association with the Indians' *temescals,* a combination sweathouse-bathing ritual involving mystical instruction by a shaman. Cabot realized, however, that the bathing was necessary to alleviate suffering from arthritis and rheumatism. The therapeutic baths later would be instrumental in the development of the town of Paso Robles.

In 1827 Cabot, at the instruction of the new Mexican governor of Alta California, Jose Maria Echeandia, made a report on the missionary possessions. He wrote of the adobe house and rancho by the beach at San Simeon, with its 800 head of cattle, horses, and breeding mares; the sheep ranch to the south at Santa Ysabel; the barley ranch at San Antonio; and the wheat ranches, each with a large adobe house, at Paso de Robles and Asuncion. What shows through in the report is that, despite a fairly harsh environment, the mission at San Miguel had become what most people of the world would regard as a paradise—albeit

Top: The Rios Caledonia Adobe in San Miguel, shown here circa 1925, was the home of Petronillo Rios. Restored by the Friends of the Adobes, today it is a public museum owned by San Luis Obispo County. The efforts of the Friends group saved this adobe from almost certain destruction. Courtesy, San Luis Obispo County Historical Museum

Bottom: The Andrews Adobe had its beginnings as a home built for the mayordomo of Mission San Luis Obispo. At one time it was owned by J.P. Andrews, whose name is still associated with it. Later owners included Mr. and Mrs. Banning Garrett (Mrs. Garrett was the founding president of the County Historical Society) and Jim Williamson and Dr. Anthony Wolfe, who restored it in the 1960s. Courtesy, San Luis Obispo County Historical Museum

Above: Mission San Miguel's outlying rancho, the Paso de Robles, was granted to Pedro Narvaez in 1844 during secularization. It eventually was bought by Daniel and James Blackburn and Lazarus Godchaux for $8,000. This adobe had been the home of Petronillo Rios, from whom the Blackburns had obtained the ranch. By 1864 they were running both sheep and cattle on Paso de Robles and Rancho Santa Margarita, which they also bought. Courtesy, Bancroft Library

Above: The Paso Robles ranch house, shown here around 1893, stood near present-day Templeton. It was used by Petronillo Rios as his ranch house after he left the Caledonia Adobe. Courtesy, Archives of the Archdiocese of Los Angeles

Facing page bottom: La Loma Adobe in San Luis Obispo was built in the late-eighteenth century as a home for Don Francisco Estevan Quintana. Owned by many families, including the Boronda, Munoz, Bowden, and Deleissegues families, it is one of the oldest adobes in the city. Courtesy, Southwest Museum, Guy Giffen Collection

with thorns.

Father Luis Antonio Martinez, the chief priest at San Luis Obispo from 1790 to 1830, could and did boast of still greater prosperity. Martinez presided over one of the most affluent of all the missions. Moreover he was a great character, among the most celebrated of all the mission clergy.

Father Martinez spent his entire missionary career at San Luis Obispo. To a large extent, the entire second, or final, phase of that mission's life as a Franciscan institution was in his hands. He was a busy, extremely capable administrator, and a man of considerable wit and sarcasm. Remarkably, despite the demands of his job, Martinez managed to stay in touch with the main political and intellectual currents of his day, including independence movements in Mexico and the rest of the Spanish colonial world. Martinez denounced each of these efforts, especially that in Mexico.

These denunciations might not have placed Martinez in jeopardy later on, had he not been

such a well-known figure. His outspokenness and sense of bravado made him one of the best-known Franciscans in California. In 1884 novelist Helen Hunt Jackson used descriptions of Martinez in developing the fictional priest who marries Allessandro and Ramona. Immortalized in the novel *Ramona*, published years after his death in 1856, Martinez helped form the stereotype of a Franciscan missionary in early California.

This earthy, jovial Franciscan was also a man of courage, as he demonstrated in 1818 when Hippolyte de Bouchard, a French-born privateer loosely affiliated with the Republic of the Plata (Argentina) and flying the Argentine flag, decided to assist the cause of Mexican independence by attacking the remote Spanish outpost in California.

Martinez sent 25 neophytes trained as soldiers to assist in retaking Monterey, which Bouchard had sacked. He personally led a group of 35 neophytes south to Santa Barbara, and from there to the scene of Bouchard's final raid at San Juan Capistrano. In return, Governor Sola commended Martinez to the viceroy, who formally thanked the priest and promised to commend him to the king in Madrid.

Rumors that Martinez had a secret gold mine near Mission San Luis Obispo were widely circulated during the "quicksilver rush" that began in the Central Coast in the 1860s. Much of this is based on the accounts of Don Jose de Jesus "Totoi"

Pio Pico was the last governor of Mexican California. His cousin, Jose de Jesus Pico, was granted the Piedras Blancas Rancho. During his last days as governor, Pico granted 87 landgrants, many of which were not confirmed by the land courts set up by the Americans in 1851. Courtesy, San Luis Obispo County Historical Museum

Pico, once owner of the Piedra Blanca Ranch (which became the property of George Hearst in 1865)—a great source of folklore, and as much a local hero as San Luis Obispo ever witnessed. These rumors helped make the priest not only a fascinating historical figure, but a magnet for trouble in the years that followed the Mexican takeover of California in 1822.

When Jose Maria Echeandia was appointed governor of California under the new Mexican Constitution of 1824, he arrived intent on secularizing the missions.

In terms of developing material resources, the missions had been a resounding success, but they had failed to develop a population of Hispanicized Native Americans that was sufficient to defend the province. Meanwhile, Alta California had become an increasingly attractive place for foreign merchants in their illicit trade for hides. These, and many other factors, combined to make California ripe for foreign annexation.

Mexico's political, economic, and social instability also was a problem. It was impossible for Echeandia, or the government he served, to justify protecting the missionaries and their wards, with all their material prosperity, when hundreds of thousands of Mexican families were starving. The new government in Mexico was anti-clerical to a large extent and the alleged wealth of a Father Luis Martinez was politically untenable. Such wealth would have to be shared with the masses who lived in misery.

Moreover, sustaining the cost of government in Alta California had a high cost. The soldiers in Monterey had not been paid for some time. In 1829 they mutinied under the leadership of Joaquin Solis, an ex-convict from Mexico, and Jose Maria Herrera, the government's financial agent at Monterey. Priests like Martinez and Cabot supported this revolt and used it to urge reunification of California under Spanish rule as a means of protecting missionary interests. Solis and Herrera were defeated by Echeandia in a confrontation at Santa Barbara.

After the failure of the Herrera-Solis rebellion, Echeandia decided to rid his province of certain priests. Martinez topped the list. On February 3, 1830, Echeandia signed a warrant for the arrest of Martinez, charging him with treason, sedition, and smuggling. The question of Martinez's complicity in the Solis-Herrera revolt is still a matter of open-ended debate among historians.

The subsequent deportation to Spain of Martinez marked a major transition in missionary fortunes along the Central Coast. With the disappearance of this strong personality, the missionary epoch was, in a de facto sense, over.

While Martinez's successors were not weak men, California had entered a period of great political turmoil. A new political order had emerged in Mexico. The Mexican officials viewed the Franciscan missionaries as a vestige of the old order that

This engraving of Captain William Goodwin Dana appeared in Myron Angel's *History of San Luis Obispo County, California*. Dana settled in Santa Barbara in 1825, became a Mexican citizen, and married Maria Josefa Carrillo. In 1837 he was granted the nearly 38,000-acre Rancho Nipomo by Governor Alvarado. Courtesy, San Luis Obispo County Historical Museum

should have disappeared years before. So, at a session of the *deputacion* (council of provincial government) on July 20, 1830, Governor Echeandia introduced a plan for converting the missions into pueblos. This plan was premature, since it did not have the approval of the Mexican government. It was also precipitous, in that it was written by a governor who had managed to alienate many influential *Californio* families and was soon to be replaced. Nonetheless, secularization was an idea whose time had come. Popular recognition of this fact destroyed the authority traditionally held by the Franciscan priests. A political vacuum developed in the mission communities. Many became wild and unmanageable—none more so than San Luis Obispo, which came to be known as the Barrio of the Tiger.

Father Ramon Abella was the last, and possibly the most unhappy, regular Franciscan at San Luis Obispo. He was both elderly (69 years of age) and in a state of poor health when he was assigned to the mission in July 1834. Yet so desperate was the need for priests that he also was obliged to take responsibility for Mission San Miguel during his final year at San Luis Obispo, 1840-1841.

Poor Father Abella had to put up with some of the most nefarious characters in the history of California. During this time large numbers of homeless immigrants from Sonora, Sinaloa, and New Mexico drifted through San Luis Obispo

County. They lingered at the mission, stole the mission's horses and mules, and sold liquor to the neophytes. When, in August 1834, Governor Jose Figueroa issued a proclamation outlining procedures for secularization of the missions, the transients saw a splendid opportunity to take over much of the mission lands.

Abella retreated to San Miguel to escape the outrages in San Luis Obispo. Matters were no better there, however. An 1837 report from the government-appointed administrator of Mission San Luis Obispo, Innocente Garcia, related how a party led by Kentucky mountain man Isaac Graham forced its way into the *monjeria* (monastery for unmarried young women), after which Garcia abolished the institution, "leaving each family to care for their women." Garcia was from New Mexico and tried to manage the mission effectively, but without success. When he raised large harvests of grain, "there was no market, and there was more food than the Indians could eat."

In 1845 Pio Pico, the last governor of Mexican California, decreed that the Indians must return to their mission lands or forfeit them. But there was nothing for the Indians to return to. So, in 1846, the mission proper was sold to Petronillo Rios, a retired Mexican artillery sergeant, and William Reed, an English sailor and lumberman. They planned to raise sheep and harvest the timber near Cambria, which was on mission

lands. The Franciscan era in San Luis Obispo was over.

In 1842, the *encargado* (administrator) at San Luis Obispo was directed to divide what remained of the mission lands into square parcels, to be distributed to the remaining Indians. Meanwhile the outlying lands of the county's two missions were divided into great ranchos. Huer-Huero Rancho, near the present-day town of Creston, was granted to Mariano Bonilla, later *alcalde* (justice of the peace) of San Luis Obispo, in 1842. The 37,888-acre Rancho Nipomo in southwestern San Luis Obispo County was awarded to a New England sea captain, William Godwin Dana, in 1837. Dana was one of many so-called "perfectos"—that is, Yankees who came to California, adopted the Roman Catholic religion, married Mexican women,

and had large families.

Isaac J. Sparks, born in Bowdoin, Maine, was another example of such a Yankee. Sparks was among the first Americans to cross the Sierra Nevada into California, arriving in Los Angeles in 1832. In 1843 Governor Manuel Micheltorena granted Sparks the 22,000-acre Rancho Huasna in south-central San Luis Obispo County.

Francisco Ziba Branch was a trapper from the Santa Fe party who came to Los Angeles with the William Wolfskill expedition in 1832. In 1835 Branch married Manuela Carlon, daughter of Zepherino Carlon, descendant of Felipe de Goycochea of Santa Barbara. Through his wife's connections, he was granted the 16,955-acre Rancho Santa Manuela by Governor Alvarado in 1837. The rancho includes the present-day commu-

nity of Arroyo Grande.

Californio families received the vast majority of the 35 Mexican land grants in what later became San Luis Obispo County. For example, the Estrada brothers, Joaquin and Julian—sons of Jose Ramon Estrada, the alcalde at Monterey—did quite well indeed. In 1842 Alvarado granted their father the 4,469-acre San Simeon, which he passed on to his son Julian. In 1841 Julian himself was granted the 13,184-acre Rancho Santa Rosa which included present-day Cambria. That same year Joaquin was granted the 17,735-acre Rancho Santa Margarita just north of the Cuesta in San Luis Obispo County.

Santa Margarita, which had been used for sowing field crops by the padres, was converted by Estrada into a cattle ranch. Virtually all of the 22 Mexican grants made in San Luis Obispo County during the period 1840 to 1846 witnessed a similar transition from agriculture to cattle raising. San Luis Obispo was becoming a "cow county," the term used for the Southern California counties that had a primarily cattle economy until after the Gold Rush.

San Luis Obispo also was seeing increased immigration. Chief among the *extranjeros* (foreigners) were John Michael Price and John Wilson.

Price, born in Bristol, England, took employment as a seaman at an early age. Like the majority of extranjeros, Price had entered California illegally. Feeling uncomfortable with their undocumented status, they sought to ingratiate themselves with certain Young Turks among the Californios.

In 1836 Isaac Graham, the Kentucky mountain man, put his troop of sharpshooters in the service of Juan B. Alvarado, president of the *deputacion*, the first real legislative assembly in the province. These riflemen joined Alvarado's Californio horsemen in overthrowing the interim Mexican governor, Nicholas Gutierrez. Alvarado got the

Below: The Isaac Sparks Adobe on Rancho Huasna was also known as the Harloe Adobe, after one of Sparks' grandsons. This adobe is the oldest in the south county. The first part of the adobe was built in 1831 by a trapper named Stone. Sparks was granted Rancho Huasna in 1843 and used Stone's adobe as the beginning of his ranch house. Courtesy, Southwest Museum, Guy Giffen Collection

Left: This mid-1890s photo of the Francisco Ziba Branch Adobe was taken by Arroyo Grande physician Dr. Edwin Paulding, and shows his niece, Ormie Paulding, in the foreground. The Branch home unfortunately has not survived. Courtesy, San Luis Obispo County Historical Museum, Paulding Collection

John Michael Price is shown here with his wife Maria Andrea Carlon Price and daughter Ramona (Sister Angelica). Price came to the county in 1836. Through hard work, he eventually purchased much of Rancho El Pismo from Isaac Sparks, including the land on which the cities of Pismo Beach and Grover City now stand. He was actively involved in politics, serving as alcalde, supervisor, and town trustee. Courtesy, San Luis Obispo County Historical Museum, Elsie Muzio Collection

deputacion to declare California a "free and sovereign state," paving the way for the first major issuance of land grants to the victors and their allies.

In 1840 Price was arrested, along with Graham and more than 60 other undocumented extranjeros. Subsequently freed, Price became *mayordomo* (steward) at Isaac Sparks' Huasna Rancho, after holding a similar position under Dana at Nipomo.

Price was also "perfected" during this time. On May 13, 1844, he married Maria Andrea Carlon, daughter of Zeferino Carlon and Maria Dominga Cota. The Cotas, a prominent Californio family, had numerous descendants and collateral relatives throughout Southern California, especially in the Ventura-Santa Barbara region— including the owners of the

45,000-acre Rancho Rio de Santa Clara at Hueneme and the 15,500-acre Santa Rosa Rancho at Buellton. Price had truly adopted the California way of life!

Coincidental to the American conquest of California, Price obtained from Sparks the 8,839-acre Rancho Pizmo, became alcalde of San Luis Obispo, member of the first county board of supervisors, and founder of Pismo Beach.

Captain John Wilson, born in Dundee, Scotland, also became a landholder in San Luis Obispo by way of perfection and married into an influential Californio family. In his case, the marriage was to Ramona Carrillo de Pacheco, the 24-year-old widow of Lieutenant Romualdo Pacheco—a prominent figure in the arrest and deportation of Father Martinez. Wilson adopted Dona Ramona's two sons, Romualdo and Mariano, and sent them to a Presbyterian missionary school at Oahu, Hawaii. Romualdo went on to become governor of California in 1875 and to serve in the United States Congress.

Rafael Villavicencio, usually called "Villa," was a Californio who received a fine grant of his own choosing. The son of an invalid Spanish soldier who settled in the newly founded pueblo of San Jose in 1797, Villa came to the Central Coast in 1838. He occupied land just north of the Cayucos Rancho. On July 24, 1842, Governor Alvarado granted Villa the 8,893-acre Rancho San Geronimo. In the meantime, Villa had received the Rancho Canada de Portezuela, about a quarter of a league (1,100 acres) in size somewhere in the Mexican District of Monterey. There is no record of this rancho, other than the original award by Governor Alvarado to Villa in 1839. Villa may have sold this rancho in the early 1840s to make improvements at the Rancho San Geronimo. These included adobe structures, a gristmill, and looms on which the wives of his native vaqueros wove blankets. Villa became a very prosperous ranchero.

There were many Californios who did not receive the generous grants issued to the extranjeros. Acceptance of their lot did not come easily. Victor Linares was one of the least fortunate. In 1842 the vast Rancho Canada de Los Osos was granted to Linares, only to be regranted

to John Wilson in April of the following year. Linares, the father of six children, had not done well in comparison with many of his Hispanic and all of his Anglo neighbors.

It is not surprising that Victor Linares' son Pio would become the most feared *bandido* of the Central Coast a decade later. By then San Luis Obispo would have fully earned its reputation as the the Barrio of the Tiger.

The Bear Flag Rebellion

Top: The Wilson Adobe on Rancho Canada de Los Osos y Pecho y Islay belonged to John Wilson, a ship's captain. Wilson was granted Rancho El Chorro, while his wife, Ramona Carrillo Pacheco, was granted Rancho Suey in addition to the Los Osos. He acquired the Huerta de Romualdo Rancho to provide access between the Chorro and Los Osos. Courtesy, San Luis Obispo County Historical Museum

Bottom: This 1930 view shows John Michael Price's "tri-gabled" adobe home and the two-story dairy/schoolhouse he built in Price Canyon. Today the City of Pismo Beach owns Price's second home, not shown in this photograph, known as the "Anniversary House." Price built this second house for his and his wife's golden wedding anniversary. Courtesy, San Luis Obispo County Historical Museum

Captain John Wilson was granted Rancho Canada de Los Osos y Pecho y Islay by Governor Pio Pico in 1845. Though the ranchos had earlier been granted to others, they were regranted to Wilson and his partner Diego Scott. Wilson was a well-respected ship's captain and was mentioned by Richard Henry Dana in *Two Years Before the Mast.* He later bought Mission San Luis Obispo, but the purchase was annulled under American law. This view of his ranch house was done by William Rich Hutton in October 1850 while Hutton was surveying Wilson's ranch. Courtesy, Huntington Library

took place at Sonoma on June 10, 1846. However, the Mexican-American War did not reach San Luis Obispo for more than six months. The American invasion of Mexican California began as a localized revolt of American-born ranchers and merchants in the Sonoma, Napa, and Sacramento valleys, whom John C. Fremont had done his best to stir to rebellion.

During the next seven months, Fremont held command of the largest American ground forces in California. Fremont captured San Diego, then returned to Monterey by ship to lead an overland expedition to San Luis Obispo and Santa Barbara. The central portion of the province was reckoned to be the most dangerous to subdue, and hence it was left to last.

The American invasion had taken the Californios off guard. American, British, and French extranjeros often had taken sides in the Californios' many civil conflicts, and while they often made the difference between victory and defeat, they had not been perceived as the enemy of the Californios' basic interests. Foreign invasion was a different matter. Although ill-prepared to fight a modern

war, the Californios made a valiant effort.

Fremont's advance south from the Monterey-Salinas Plain was seen by the Californios as their last chance to avoid extermination. Many rancheros, like "Totoi" Pico, returned to the fray.

Pico, mentioned earlier as a source of folklore regarding Father Luis Martinez's secret gold mine, was arrested by Fremont's forces at Los Osos on December 14, 1846. Although sentenced to death by a court martial, Pico was pardoned by Fremont, who took him to Los Angeles as a prisoner. Whatever Fremont's motives, his generosity of spirit greatly impressed the Californios; Pico himself became a lifelong friend and supporter of Fremont. Shortly thereafter, the Capitulation of Cahuenga ended all formal hostilities in California.

The state may well have been delivered from additional months of bloody guerrilla warfare by this event, which has since become a San Luis Obispo legend.

From 1846 to 1850, the year California officially became a state, local government in San Luis Obispo took on an ad hoc character because of the ineffectiveness of the interim military government. During that same period, a major shift took place in the political and economic geography of America's new possession on the Pacific shore.

"Southern California"—beginning just south of Monterey County along the coast, and at the Tehachapis in the interior

—was the vital economic core of the province after 1820. Following the Gold Rush, however, this portion of the state became wild and remote, avoided by most travelers and neglected by the legislators in Sacramento, who came mainly from San Francisco and the Mother Lode country. This remained true until after 1869. It took a whole generation for institutions based on American-style law to grow and become accepted along the Central Coast.

During the mid-1850s, the El Camino Real between San Jose and San Diego was a deserving successor to the Natchez Trace and other early American byways as the "most lawless trail in the West," according to newspaper accounts of the day. Despite this unsavory reputation, Henry Miller, a fine artist, travel commentator, and diarist,

decided to travel this route in 1856, evidently for sightseeing purposes.

Miller was not favorably impressed by San Luis Obispo, saying that

the Mission [has] metamorphosed into a little town of about 150 houses, inhabited principally by natives and Mexicans; however quite a number of Americans have also settled here . . . After breakfast, I took a ramble about the mission buildings, some of which are in ruins, though once remarkably strong, constructed of rock joined with very hard cement. In the building adjoining the Church is held court at present, in the absence of a better one . . . I was informed by a young and very intelligent American that the American government was very badly sustained here and a jury could not be found to convict a criminal . . .

Top: Dr. W.W. Hays was San Luis Obispo's first permanent doctor. Arriving here in 1866, he was instrumental in founding the County Hospital and County Medical Association. He was born in 1838 in Maryland. Courtesy, San Luis Obispo County Historical Museum

Bottom: In 1873 the new county courthouse was finished. Replacing William G. Dana's Casa Grande, it was an imposing neo-classical structure with the sheriff's office and jail in the basement. It cost $42,000 to build and was in use until 1939. The Hall of Records is in the background. Courtesy, San Luis Obispo County Historical Museum

The "young and very intelligent American" was probably Walter Murray. Of Anglo-Scottish origin, Murray was a journalist who in 1869 founded the first permanent newspaper in California, the *San Luis Obispo Tribune.* In addition, Murray served as a District Court judge and led the 1858 Committee of Vigilance, which handed out death sentences to many of the more lawless elements in the county. More than any other individual, Murray helped tame the Barrio of the Tiger.

Murray recognized that the county would never grow and prosper while crime and banditry were rampant. By 1853 Jack Powers, a personal nemesis of Murray, had allied himself with feared bandido Pio Linares. Together, along with fel-low bandido Joaquin Valenzuela, the two embarked upon a series of bloodthirsty robberies and cattle thefts.

Ironically it was Murray whom Powers retained as defense counsel in 1853, when one of his associates was arrested for murder. As a lawyer, Murray believed in an adequate defense for all accused criminals. Before a jury of nine Californios and three Yankees—with "Totoi" Pico as foreman—Murray won an acquittal.

Emboldened by the verdict, the Powers-Linares-Valenzuela gang resumed its activities. In response to the outrage of the Anglo population, Murray and a group of Americans—including Daniel Blackburn, future co-founder of Paso Robles—met at Murray's adobe.

The French Hotel stood across Monterey Street from Mission San Luis Obispo. This building stood on the site of an earlier structure and was destroyed in a fire in 1908. In a room on the second story, Walter Murray died from peritonitis on October 5, 1875. Courtesy, San Luis Obispo County Historical Museum

Top: The *Daily Republic,* founded by Myron Angel, was San Luis Obispo's first daily newspaper, beginning its daily service three months before the *Tribune* did. The paper lasted only until 1890. This building is the Shaw House on Morro Street between Marsh and Higuera. Courtesy, San Luis Obispo County Historical Museum

Bottom: Pio Linares was a noted bandito. The son of Victor Linares, he was coleader of the Powers-Linares gang which terrorized the countryside during the 1850s. Sought by the Committee of Vigilance, which was formed to fight the gang, he was killed in 1858 in a shootout near what is today Turri Road and Los Osos Valley Road. Courtesy, San Luis Obispo County Historical Museum

The group might never have developed into a committee of vigilance if Pio Linares had not responded to the threat posed by this meeting. Hearing of the meeting, Linares led a gang of his followers to Murray's home. His plan was to shoot through the windows, killing Murray and Blackburn. His comrades, however, lost their nerve at the last moment.

Eventually 148 men signed the roll forming the Committee of Vigilance. Sixty-two of the names were Spanish; clearly, the Californios also had come to the end of their tether with regard to the endemic lawlessness of the Barrio of the Tiger.

The "justice" of the Committee was swift and violent. They immediately built a makeshift outdoor courtroom and gallows, and their first "official" act was to successfully try and execute Joaquin Valenzuela. Before the Committee was finished, more would meet the same fate—including the associate of Powers who had been acquitted only a year before, and who now met his death at the hands of an extralegal tribunal of which his former defense attorney was a part.

Thus San Luis Obispo, with the legal services of Walter Murray, became a fit place to raise an American family—legal technicalities and all.

Port San Luis, Gateway to the World

For years the Central Coast was without a good natural harbor. This led to many difficulties that interfered with the development of adequate transportation services. Sometimes the results were comic—such as when Walter Murray arrived in San Luis Bay in 1853. The small boat rowing him ashore capsized in the powerful surf. The ship's captain, instead of trying to help Murray, who was up to his neck in water, simply threw him the leather bags of mail and said, "Here, you take this to town!" There also could be tragic consequences of the lack of portside facilities: The previous year, Senator Henry Tefft, William G. Dana's son-in-law and a signatory of the California State Constitution, drowned in rough waters while trying to swim ashore from his sailing vessel.

Early on, the proximity of the future county seat to San Luis Bay seems to have forecast its role as the major harbor of the Central Coast.

The establishment of Mission San Luis Obispo de Tolosa on September 1, 1772, gave lasting importance to San Luis Creek as a gateway to the sea for the

San Miguel Farmer's Union is seen here around 1890. Farmers in the county opposed construction of the San Luis Obispo & Santa Maria Valley Railroad, fearing the rise of a monopoly. Courtesy, San Luis Obispo County Historical Museum

prosperous mission economy. Mission-era documents suggest that contact between oceangoing vessels and the mission some 10 miles upstream was established prior to 1794. Pioneer California historian Hubert Howe Bancroft reported how the "friars were commended in 1805 for their cool reception of a foreign vessel, probably the *Lelia Byrd*, which came in pretended need for fresh provisions, but really in quest for opportunities for illicit trade."

tive of Boston's Bryant, Sturgis & Co., could not help but be amused by the salty "seaman's English" of Father Luis Gil y Taboada, the priest who had recently taken charge of the mission—language no doubt acquired from the reverend father's participation in illicit trade at his previous assignment at Mission Santa Cruz.

The Avila Adobe, which stood at the mouth of San Luis Creek until after the Second World War, in all probability was begun as part of the assistencia at Rancho San Miguelito. Numerous outbuildings associated with the mission-era operation were later converted to private use.

The 1830s witnessed the decline and ultimate secularization of the mission lands. The Mexican government had no interest in maintaining the prosperity of the Spanish-born Franciscans. Gil y Toboada reported in December 1830 that the "ranch and buildings of San Miguelito are destroyed." The severely depreciated value of buildings near the mouth of San Luis Obispo Creek is confirmed by an inventory of all the assets of Mission San Luis Obispo, prepared on December 13, 1836. No valuated properties are listed for the Rancho San Miguelito.

The economic value of the area was recognized by Miguel Avila, who on March 1, 1839, petitioned the governor of California, Juan B. Alvarado, for two square leagues (5.26 square miles) of land lying around San Luis Bay. Governor Alvarado de-

The California Southern Overland Stage Company was begun in the early 1860s to serve passenger traffic along the coast. This stage stop, believed to have been at the foot of the Cuesta, is shown in an 1864 sketch by Edward Vischer. Courtesy, Bancroft Library

In 1808 a granary was built at the beach or port of San Luis Obispo to store the produce of the Rancho de Playa, renamed the Rancho San Miguelito. The dimensions were 40 varas in length and 12 varas in width (155 by 34 feet). This seems to have been the beginning of a series of permanent structures for the mission *assistencia* (assistant mission). Alfred Robinson, an American trader who arrived in California in 1829 as the resident representa-

creed that Avila was the owner of the land, but there was no formal grant for the Rancho San Miguelito until May 10, 1842. Avila was the son of a Spanish soldier stationed at the presidio of Santa Barbara. He became a member of the *escolte* (mission guard) at San Luis Obispo in 1824. He quarreled with Father Martinez and was transferred to Monterey. In 1826, he married into the influential Pico family which gave him sufficient influence to gain the San Miguelito grant in 1842. He became alcalde of San Luis Obispo in 1849.

There were two unusual provisions associated with the San Miguelito grant. First, since the grant encompassed the bay, a strip along the shore 500 varas (approximately one-quarter mile) wide must remain open for public use. Second, no part of this grant must be closer than one and one-half leagues from the structures adjoining the mission complex in San Luis Obispo. Governor Pio Pico appended another provision to the granting of an additional square league in 1846: that a cart road be allowed to remain open to the port.

In 1841 Avila built an adobe house some 1,000 varas from the shore of the port. He kept about 200 head of cattle,

Top: The Mallagh Adobe in Arroyo Grande was built by Captain David Mallagh and stood just above the site of Arroyo Grande High School. It housed the south county's first school taught by David Newsome in the early 1860s. Mallagh later built Mallagh's Landing, the first wharf in the county. Courtesy, Southwest Museum, Guy Giffen Collection

Bottom: Cave Landing (known today as Pirates Cove, although it was never used by pirates), was the site of the first wharf in San Luis Obispo County. Built by Captain David P. Mallagh, the wharf served the county in the 1850s and 1860s. The site became a favorite landing for illegal alcohol during Prohibition. Courtesy, San Luis Obispo County Historical Museum

53

raised horses and sheep, and grew several acres of corn, wheat, and vegetables. Avila may well have been among the first of the Californios to engage in dairying as early as 1842. His successes during the Mexican period were based on family connections. His uncle was Jose Maria Avila—perhaps the most colorful of all the Californios—who died in a blaze of heroism at the internecine Battle of Cahuenga Pass in 1831. Moreover, Avila was married to Governor Pico's niece, Maria Inocenta.

In 1849, after the American conquest, Avila was elected alcalde of San Luis Obispo. Because of his distance from town, he resigned the position a year later. He died in 1874 under what the San Luis Obispo Tribune labeled "mysterious circumstances." He left the remains of his estates to his widow and sons. This included a second adobe in the hills above the port. Only traces of this adobe remain, northwest of the present lighthouse.

Like all the Californios, Avila suffered heavy losses during the drought of 1863-1864. In 1867 his son, Don Miguel, laid out the town of Avila and sold lots to settlers and businessmen. These merchants included a group led by John Harford, of the lumber firm of Schwartz, Harford and Co.; the Goldtree Brothers; and A. Blochman & Co., of San Luis Obispo and San Francisco.

Together these merchants formed a syndicate called the Peoples Wharf Company in De-

cember 1868. They constructed an 1,800-foot wharf just south of the mouth of San Luis Creek, approximately 100 yards south of the present-day Avila Pier. A narrow-gauge, horse-drawn railway was laid on the wharf to bring cargo inland.

The Peoples Wharf was designed to compete with Captain David P. Mallagh's Landing, built at the foot of the bluff over what nowadays is referred to as Pirates' Cove. There, in 1855, a short wharf was constructed near the natural caves often associated with the Franciscan priests' illicit trading activities during the mission era. Mallagh's Landing was often called Cave Landing. The area has no known association with pirates—not even the privateer Hippolyte de Bouchard, who sailed by Point Buchon, well out at sea, in November 1818.

A freight elevator was used to transfer cargo and passengers up and down the bluff. Mallagh purchased the operation in 1864 and promptly improved both the wharf and the road connecting the town of Avila to the main highway leading into the pueblo of San Luis Obispo. By 1868 Mallagh was doing moderately well. All of California was anticipating an economic boom when the transcontinental railway was completed as scheduled the next year. The Peoples Wharf syndicate hoped to take away his business by offering a more preferable deep-water landing in San Luis Bay.

The hoped-for boom never

happened. Instead California went into a recession partly caused by excessive speculation. Moreover, Mallagh had a contract with the packet steamers for their passenger business. Naturally the steamers wanted to take care of their freight business while they were landing passengers. The partners quarreled. In November 1872, Blochman sued the Goldtrees, and the presiding judge ordered the company dissolved. The holdings were sold at auction in front of the warehouse on the beach.

Harford managed to remain free of the major elements of the Peoples Wharf management fight. His chief interest was lumber, and the coastal schooners bringing lumber always tied up at the Peoples Wharf. He recognized that San Luis Obispo was destined to grow, especially given the importance of the newly established dairying enterprise throughout the coastal zone. The only efficient way to bring lumber into this relatively treeless region was by sea. That would be the case for the next quarter century. As early as 1871 he had decided to go ahead with a wharf of his own on the rocky shoals off Point San Luis.

While he planned for this development, he also managed to turn the legally defunct Peoples Wharf into a profit-making operation. Together with Captain John Ingalls of the Pacific mail steamer Orizaba, Harford organized a pooled bid for the assets of the Peoples Wharf at the public auction. He then convinced Mallagh to accept the po-

Left: A Chinese funeral was photographed in San Luis Obispo in the mid-1880s. The impact of the Chinese population on the county cannot be underestimated, for they built roads, wharfs, and railways. The Chinatown area of San Luis Obispo was active and vital from 1875 until the 1940s. Courtesy, San Luis Obispo County Historical Museum

Right: Ah Louis, the unofficial "Mayor of Chinatown," was photographed here circa 1920. Louis came to the county in 1869 and worked as a cook for the French Hotel. Within the next few years, on the advice of Captain John Harford, he began working as a labor contractor. He later started the first brickyard in the county and was involved in the early seed industry. A well-respected member of the community, he died in 1936 at the age of 98. Courtesy, San Luis Obispo County Historical Museum

sition of manager of the Peoples Wharf. As a result Mallagh abandoned his cumbersome landing operation and all the ships used the Peoples Wharf. The wasteful competition was over for the time being.

Harford's new wharf was completed in 1875. It extended 540 feet from the rock-strewn shore, into water averaging 15 feet in depth. He constructed a 15-pound horse rail from the wharf to Mallagh's road to the main highway. Most of the actual construction was undertaken by Chinese labor gangs, supervised by Wong On, nicknamed "Ah Louis" by Harford, who formed a long-lasting working arrangement with this Chinese man who grew into lasting prominence in San Luis Obispo County.

Harford's work coincided with a fare war between rival Pacific Coast shipping agents. A first-class fare between San Francisco and San Diego, meals included, dropped to a mere $5. There was a proportionate decrease in fare structure for intermediate points. Freight prices also were lowered. Harford boasted in the *San Luis Obispo*

Tribune that he had lowered the cost of shipping outbound freight by 50 cents per ton.

Harford's success attracted the attention of investors up and down the Pacific Coast. Despite a statewide depression, which had arrested the supply of investment capital in San Francisco, businessmen were on the lookout for "good buys" in Central and Southern California. William W. Chapman, William W. Stowe, and Henry B. Tichenor formed a syndicate called the San Luis Obispo Railroad on January 30, 1873. They appointed three San Luis Obispo County residents to the board of directors: William L. Beebe, Harford's partner in the lumber trade; Charles W. Dana, one of the numerous heirs to the 38,000-

Top: Pacific Coast Railway Engine Number 6 was shipped around the Horn, arriving in the county in December 1883. In 1894 it was converted from a wood-burning engine to a coal-burning engine. It blew up in the San Luis Obispo PCR yard in 1904 and was scrapped. Courtesy, San Luis Obispo County Historical Museum

Bottom: The Pacific Coast Railway depot at Arroyo Grande is seen here in 1883. The coming of the PCR fueled the growth of Arroyo Grande, which became a railhead for the surrounding farmland. The road in the foreground is today's Branch Street, and the view is taken from about where Paulding Intermediate School is today. Courtesy, San Luis Obispo County Historical Museum

Facing page: This circa-1890 photo shows the George Freeman Ranch on San Bernardo Creek, near Morro Bay. Unamuno, the first European to land in San Luis Obispo County in 1585, thought that this fertile land was worthless. Farmers in the late-nineteenth century proved him wrong. Courtesy, San Luis Obispo County Historical Museum

acre Rancho Nipomo and a prominent civic leader; and Edgar W. Steele, cofounder of the modern dairying industry in San Luis Obispo. Eventually the railway was to traverse the entire holdings of both the Dana family and the Steele Brothers' Corral de Piedra ranch. The group proposed to build a steam rail line running from the terminus of Captain Harford's horse-drawn line at the mouth of San Luis Creek and the town of San Luis Obispo.

The project remained dormant for over a year because of the short supply of investment capital. Then on March 2, 1874, State Senator William J. Graves introduced legislation authorizing the construction of

the San Luis Obispo & Santa Maria Valley Railroad, which was to run from San Luis Bay to the Santa Maria Valley and eventually to Santa Barbara. The grangers along the proposed route all fought the bill, claiming that it would promote a monopoly stranglehold on the farmers' grain shipments similar to that held by the Southern Pacific in the San Joaquin Valley. The governor signed the bill despite the grangers' objections.

San Francisco businessman Charles Goodall, backer of the Santa Maria Rail Road syndicate, had ample financing. He posed a genuine threat to the San Luis Obispo Rail Road promoters. In the end Harford had little choice but to sell his wharf and horse-drawn railway to Goodall for $30,000. When Goodall began construction of a line parallel to the San Luis Railroad's unbuilt line, a "paper" right-of-way, that group agreed to merge. Interestingly, while track continued to be laid, there was still no steam locomotive pre-

sent in the Central Coast until November 8, 1875.

On August 17, 1876, the first railroad run between San Luis Obispo and the wharf at San Luis Bay was made. The line was almost immediately profitable. The horse track from Avila to the end of the wharf was replaced with 42-pound (to the yard), 36-inch, narrow-gauge track, so that trains could travel directly from San Luis Obispo to the end of the now lengthened, 1,500-foot wharf. The first service to the wharf's end commenced on December 11, 1876.

The Ocean Hotel was constructed by eager investors on the curved shelf of land extending out to the entrance of the wharf. It was intended to serve passengers awaiting the frequently delayed coastal steam-

ers. The hotel failed to make money until it was resold in 1882 to Luigi Marre and Antonio Gagliardo.

Marre was the son of a Genoa innkeeper. Born in 1840, he emigrated to San Francisco in 1854. In 1879 he leased a portion of the Pecho grant from Ramona Hilliard, who had inherited the Pecho y Islay and Santa Fe ranchos from Captain John Wilson. In 1881 he married Angelina Marre, a cousin. The couple took up residence in the so-called Pecho Adobe, located where the proposed Pecho Creek Access Trail intersects Pecho Creek. The adobe is now in ruins and little remains. It probably was once a mission-era vista for the San Miguelito rancho. Later it was used by Wilson's ranch crew.

Marre purchased 6,500 acres

of the San Miguelito ranch from John Avila and John Harford, at the same time acquiring the Ocean Hotel, which he operated with Gagliardo. The partners made a success of the establishment by featuring multicourse Italian meals, attracting residents from San Luis Obispo who would pay one dollar to ride the railroad to the wharf for a weekend treat. The name of the Ocean Hotel was changed to the Hotel Marre. It was during the economic boom of the 1880s that tourists were first attracted to the area in and about San Luis Bay.

The area's vulnerability to violent Pacific storms became apparent during the winter of 1878. High tides and hurricane-force winds destroyed the Peoples Wharf, and torrential rains washed out sections of the rail-

Top: In the nineteenth century many companies were formed to quarry asphalt for use in floors and streets. This company at Avila was photographed around 1908. Other uses for asphalt included generating gas for San Luis Obispo's gaslights. Courtesy, San Luis Obispo County Historical Museum

Bottom: This spur of the Pacific Coast Railway at the Bishop's Peak Quarry provided transportation for the granite from the quarry. Courtesy, San Luis Obispo County Historical Museum

road. John Harford's vision of a safe siting for his wharf was vindicated, however. The 1,500-foot wharf survived intact.

By 1883, under the heading "Railroad Gossip," the *San Luis Obispo Tribune* described Port Harford as a

harbor of easy access, and the steamer captains regard it as the best of the second class harbors on the coast. A large strong wharf, only surpassed in California by the Oakland Ferry landing, and capable of receiving half a dozen steamers and ships at once, is the beginning of the railroad.

By 1883 the wharf was 80 feet in width and had been extended to over 3,000 feet in length.

On December 25, 1887, a fire destroyed the Port Harford warehouse, 11 railcars, and 500 feet of the wharf itself. It was a critical setback since, in the previous November, the railroad, now renamed the Pacific Coast Railway, had been extended as far south as Los Olivos in the Santa Ynez Valley. The line provided an outlet for the rich agricultural produce of the Los Osos, Edna, Huasna, Arroyo Grande, Los Berros, Nipomo, Santa Maria, Los Alamos, and Santa Ynez districts, encompassing over 300,000 acres of wheat, barley, beans, peas, and dairying land.

Right: These men were building retaining walls on Monterey Street in San Luis Obispo at the turn of the century. This photo dates from before 1909 when quarrying on Bishop's Peak was halted by ordinance. Bishop's Peak granite was used in many retaining walls and curbs throughout the city, and was used to build four buildings, three of which still stand today. This wall is in front of the Leitcher Adobe. Courtesy, San Luis Obispo County Historical Museum

Left: Bishop's Peak quarry operated for many years, providing a very hard gray granite for curbs, retaining walls, and foundations. Four buildings in the city of San Luis Obispo were built of this stone, three of which still stand. Courtesy, San Luis Obispo County Historical Museum

The rock for the Port San Luis breakwater was hauled to the port by the Pacific Coast Railway which ran flatcars out onto Harford's Wharf, from which the rock was transferred to the barge by a donkey engine. Courtesy, San Luis Obispo County Historical Museum

The dairying industry established by the Steele Brothers in the Edna Valley during the late 1860s was now thriving. The dairy farmers were dependent upon the wharf to ship their great quantities of cheese and butter to market in San Francisco. Mineral exports from the region had become important. Bituminous rock (oil-bearing shale for producing manufactured gas and for paving), asphalt, chrome, and chromite were mined or quarried along the Pacific Coast Railway, and had no other access to markets. By November 15, 1883, the average monthly shipment of asphalt amounted to 1,000 tons. The entire Central Coast relied on the wharf for lumber, iron, and machinery imports.

Because of their significance, the wharf and warehouse were quickly rebuilt. The fire drew attention to the critical role played by Port San Luis in the commercial development of the re-

gion. But the coastal access was a risky proposition. The rocky shoals off Point Buchon presented a significant maritime hazard. There was no lighthouse between Point Arguello and Piedras Blancas. Over a hundred miles of rugged California coastline was without a beacon. The point was brought home on April 30, 1888, when the large ocean steamer *Queen of the Pacific* began to take on water from a valve accidentally left open in one of its holds. The badly listing vessel searched by night for the harbor, docked at the wharf, then sank. A maritime disaster had narrowly been averted. Increased congressional pressure caused the United States Lighthouse Service to seek funding for a lighthouse at the harbor entrance.

The sum of $50,000 was appropriated in the 1888 congressional budget, and a 30-acre site on the bluffs above the harbor was designated for the build-

ing of the Port San Luis Lighthouse. A redwood structure with Prairie-Victorian styling was finally completed in the spring of 1890.

Port San Luis acquired greater economic significance in 1903 when oil production began in the Santa Maria basin. The Pacific Coast Railway was not equipped to transport liquid petroleum, so Union Oil superintendent E.W. Clark had standard-gauge rail tanks shipped up from San Pedro and remounted on narrow-gauge rolling stock. Within a month, the little railway had 35 oil-tank cars. Pacific Coast Oil, a subsidiary of Standard Oil of New Jersey, constructed a storage tank at Port Harford and began regular rail shipments from its fields near Graciosa.

The 1890s were a period of nationwide depression. Port San Luis experienced reduced business during most of the decade, and only sluggish growth during the best years. It was given a new lease on life by the oil industry. In 1906 the United States Customs Service designated it as a Port of Entry. This allowed international shipping to use the pier, particularly for petroleum shipments.

In 1906 the Union Oil Company completed a six-inch pipeline from the Santa Maria fields to Port San Luis, where the company built tanks capable of storing a quarter of a million barrels of black gold. In 1909 Union Oil management, faced with swelling production in its San Joaquin Valley fields, made a joint agreement with the Inde-

pendent Oil Producers Agency, forming a syndicate called the Producers Transportation Company. The PTC undertook the construction of a 2,450-mile-long, eight-inch pipeline from the valley fields to Avila. This was the largest oil pipeline project prior to the First World War. Moving this river of oil required 15 pumping stations along the route just to keep the petroleum moving. Field storage for 27 million barrels of oil had to be created at a tank farm in San Luis Obispo, as well as new wharf facilities at Port San Luis. The project cost $4.5 million—one million dollars above the original estimates. The project was accomplished un-

Top: Oilport was built by the California Petroleum Company, Limited. Finished in 1907, it suffered financial losses and operated for less than 30 days. A storm, which the bankrupt owners called a "tidal wave," destroyed its wharf. It stood where Sunset Palisades is today. Courtesy, San Luis Obispo County Historical Museum

Bottom: This circa-1910 view shows the Marre Hotel and Harford's Wharf with the extension built for oil tankers. This extension was used until the construction of the Union Oil Wharf. Courtesy, San Luis Obispo County Historical Museum

Top: The visit of the Great White Fleet to Port San Luis on April 30, 1908, caused great excitement. The Pacific Coast Railway ran special excursion trains to Avila to bring in spectators. Courtesy, San Luis Obispo County Historical Museum

Bottom: The Mess Detail, Battery E-251, Coast Artillery was photographed in 1933. The strategic importance of the Port San Luis oil facilities was recognized by the government during World War I, at which time the Coast Artillery was assigned to guard them. Courtesy, San Luis Obispo County Historical Museum

der severe time constraints—the business community sensed war fever. The first pipe was laid on July 29, 1909, and the first oil poured out at Port San Luis in March 1910.

Union Oil later acquired all of the Petroleum Transportation Company stock and became sole owners of the pipeline.

The geopolitical significance of Port San Luis was given full rec-

ognition on April 30, 1908, when President Theodore Roosevelt's Great White Fleet anchored offshore, enroute from San Diego and San Pedro to San Francisco via Monterey. Two thousand local residents took the Pacific Coast Railway out to the beach to view the fleet.

The strategic vulnerability of San Luis Obispo County became an issue during both world wars because of the oil shipment facilities at Port San Luis. From 1917 to 1918 a full company of infantry was stationed at the Union Oil Tank Farm operation in San Luis Obispo, while units of the Coast Artillery guarded the Point San Luis-Point Buchon area. Artillery and cavalry units also patrolled the cliffs and beaches during the panic-stricken days following the attack on Pearl Harbor. Between 90 and 300 men reinforced the Coast Guard detachment at the lighthouse, from 1941 to 1943.

Port San Luis Lighthouse, Then and Now

The Port San Luis Lighthouse is the best-preserved example of a stick-style lighthouse on the West Coast. Photo by Tim Olson

The Port San Luis Lighthouse, the second in San Luis Obispo County, was built to serve the coastal trade with the connection to the Pacific Coast Railway at Port Harford. The brick foundation was constructed from local bricks, manufactured in the brickyard of Ah Louis in San Luis Obispo. A "fourth order" Fresnel lens, a design providing brighter intensity than earlier lenses, was manufactured in 1878 by Sautter Levonnier et Cie in Paris. The lighthouse was automated in 1974, and on March 30, 1976, the lens was transported to the San Luis Obispo County Museum, where it has continuously been on display.

Sound signals also were used at the lighthouse site. Initially a bell was used, then a steam whistle, and finally, a series of air horn devices. The compressor used for the air horns between 1899 and 1974 remains in the signal or horn building southwest of the lighthouse. The interior of the structure has elegant Victorian Craftsman trusses. The circa-1890 signal flagpole with its crossbeam survived the heavy winter storms in 1983, but had to be taken down for safety reasons in 1984.

The lighthouse area is without natural springs or creek run-off. From the time of the lighthouse opening, its staff was dependent on either water that was carried to the site, or captured rainwater. Two large cisterns are located to the east of the lighthouse, with a large cement collecting field on the slope northeast of the cisterns. A modern well supplements the supplies with non-potable water.

The lighthouse, keeper's house, signal horn building, and other facilities still stand and are being preserved for use as a possible museum of lighthouse history along the Pacific.

CHAPTER 5

Dairies, Rails, and County Roads

I n the years immediately following the actions of the Committee of Vigilance (1858), San Luis Obispo began the slow process of evolving as an American town. This evolution—of great importance to the American West—nearly took place prematurely.

In 1859 the counties of Southern California resented being slighted by the government in Sacramento, which was dominated by the more populous counties of the goldfield districts and the San Francisco Bay Area. The influential Pico family made arrangements to have the six southernmost counties secede from the state to form the "Territory of California." Pico selected San Luis Obispo as the territorial capital. The planned secession was averted by the greater tensions that culminated in the Civil War. By the time that conflict ended, the railroad era had arrived in California. San Luis Obispo, however, did not have a mainline railroad connection until 1894, nor did it possess a through connection to both San Francisco and Los Angeles until January 1901. Between 1860 and the pre-railroad boom of the 1880s, the county

The last "railfan" trip on the Pacific Coast Railway was run on November 8, 1940. This view shows the train passing the Southern Pacific railyard, with the Southern Pacific Roundhouse in the background. Courtesy, Anthony Thompson

Right: In 1864 German-born artist Edward Vischer drew San Luis Obispo as he found it, with San Luis Mountain in the background. Reeling from two years of drought, the county's ranchos were on the brink of a new era. Power based on land ownership was about to change with the influx of new money and new settlers. Courtesy, Bancroft Library

Above: George Steele, shown here around 1875, was active with his brothers in bringing the dairying industry to San Luis Obispo County. Courtesy, San Luis Obispo County Historical Museum

reverted to a sleepy backwater.

A basic economic change took place between 1862 and 1865. In what appeared to be a complete disaster, virtually all of the herds of mission-bred cattle and sheep were destroyed in the great drought of 1862-1864. The two rainless years killed as many as 300,000 head of cattle and 100,000 sheep. Visitors to the area remarked that the sun-bleached bones of dead cattle were strewn over every hill and gully. An almost blinding effect was created by the late afternoon sun as it reflected off the chalk-white skeletal remains in the old mission pasture, the *El Portrero de San Luis Obispo*—now the Cal Poly campus just north of the town. Virtually all of the *Californio* families were ruined. The drought marked the end of rancho days along the Central Coast.

Within a year, Anglo-American entrepreneurs had arrived in the county to buy up the bankrupt ranchos. In 1865 Joseph Hubbard Hollister—brother of

Colonel W.W. Hollister, who had developed the California sheep industry at his famed San Justo Ranch in what is now San Benito County—bought the Chorro and San Luisito ranchos. Lands in the Chorro Valley, once belonging to the Quintana and Canet families and to Captain John Wilson, now served as pasture for Hollister sheep. The area later became Camp San Luis Obispo, a portion of which is used by Cuesta College and the California Men's Colony.

In the following year, 1866, a still more significant change took place. Edgar Willis Steele and his brothers, wealthy dairymen who owned the Pescadero Ranch in San Mateo County, purchased 45,000 acres of land in the southern Edna Valley. The owners had been ruined by the drought. They paid approximately $1.10 an acre for the Corral de Piedra, Pismo, Bolsa de Chamizal (now Chamisal), and Arroyo Grande ranchos, calling them "cow heaven." The rains

The Rodriguez Adobe is the last standing structure associated with the Corral de Piedra Rancho. It was continuously occupied until 1986, but its future is now uncertain. It was owned by Henry A. Tefft, San Luis Obispo's delegate to the State Constitutional Convention of 1849 and the county's first district judge, before Tefft's tragic drowning in 1852 at Port San Luis. Courtesy, San Luis Obispo County Historical Museum

had returned, the grass was tall and green, and the price was ideal for these investors, accustomed as they were to the higher land prices of the Bay Area.

The Corral de Piedra, however, proved to be something less than a bargain. The Villavincencio family's title to the 30,911-acre rancho proved to be defective. The Steeles became involved in two decades of costly litigation over the matter and ultimately had to pay a $150,000 judgment—nearly three times the amount paid originally for all four ranches. The judgment was ultimately their financial undoing, but only after they had demonstrated that the Central Coast was indeed "cow heaven."

The Steeles stocked their dairylands with more than 600 head of first-register milk cows. They employed over 100 men to build fences and milking sheds, and to harvest hayfields. Their experience in dairying attracted other farmers. By 1887 the San Luis Obispo Board of Trade boasted that the county had surpassed even Marin County as the "banner cow country" of California.

In one experiment undertaken with 150 milking stock over a three-day period, Edgar W. Steele produced a pound of butter with every 17.76 pounds of milk and a pound of cheese with every 8.75 pounds of milk. The statewide average was 25 pounds of milk for every pound of butter and 10 for a pound of cheese!

The Steeles' specialty was cheese. They divided their property into five dairies, with approximately 150 cows on each. They built 50 to 60 miles of board fences to corral the cows on the rich feed lands. As early as 1870, the San Francisco-based *Commercial Herald*, the standard commercial and credit reporter for the West, valued the Steeles' holdings at $150 million.

In 1868 Ira Van Gordon purchased over 4,000 acres of the San Simeon Rancho, stocking it with 200 head of high-grade milkers and building a spacious home on San Simeon Creek. The Van Gordon holdings were soon coveted by George

Top: The Swiss-American Supply Company in Cambria is shown here in the early 1900s. The influence of the Italian-Swiss in the county was strong, especially in dairying. The Italian-Swiss came to the county as impoverished immigrants in the 1870s and 1880s, and by the 1890s their hard work had paid off. Courtesy, San Luis Obispo County Historical Museum

Bottom: The love many of the county's immigrants felt for the United States was amply demonstrated by Fourth of July celebrations. This view shows the Chiesa Restaurant, which stood on Monterey near Chorro, decorated for a celebration. The Chiesas were Italian-Swiss immigrants. Courtesy, San Luis Obispo County Historical Museum

They operated it under the name of Excelsior Cheese Factory, producing at "the astonishing rate of 1,200 pounds [of cheese] a day from a total of 9,000 pounds of milk." This operation eventually became the Harmony Valley Creamery.

The attractive production statistics attracted other experienced dairymen, like Morgan Brians from Sonoma County. He moved his operations into Green Valley, just north of Harmony, in 1871. He milked 165 first-register cows, devoted exclusively to butter production.

The high quantity and grade of milk production could not be sustained throughout the year. The statistics increased during the so-called "green months" of March through June, when production peaked. Things were not so easy during the remainder of the year. Making a go of dairying along the county's north coast would take stalwart farmers as well as good stock.

Hearst, who had purchased the massive Piedra Blanca Rancho in 1865.

Cheese makers from the dairy counties of upstate New York began to move into the region. During the autumn of 1869, the partnership of Ivans and Everett established a cheese factory on the southern part of the Santa Rosa Rancho. The operation was purchased by Bower and Black in 1871.

Cinnabar or mercury mining was a major industry in the mountains between Cambria and Paso Robles for much of the late-nineteenth and early-twentieth centuries. This view shows some of the operations at the Oceanic Mine north of Cambria. Courtesy, San Luis Obispo County Historical Museum

The joint stock company of Bowen & Baker, Leffingwell, Mathers, Campbell, Scott, Phelan, Gillespie, and Whitaker, operating under the name B.F. Mayfield, also purchased dairy ranches in the north coast region near San Simeon and Santa Rosa creeks. Like the Steeles in the Edna Valley, these ranches employed newly arrived immigrants, including Portuguese from the Azores and Italian Swiss from the cantons adjacent to the newly unified nation of Italy.

These immigrants had excellent backgrounds in farming. The Azores were suffering from overpopulation, complicated by the damage wrought by dozens of massive earthquakes that had occurred since the 1840s. The Italian Swiss suffered from the economic dislocations of the risorgimento. The bulk of their cheese trade had been with the Austrian provinces of Lombardy and Venetia. When the Italian nation absorbed

these regions, tariff walls were erected, cutting off those markets. Thousands of Portuguese and Italian Swiss came to the coastal counties of California, which closely resembled areas like the Azores and Canton Ticino. Both groups possessed the requisite skills for dairy farming and cheese making.

Names like Tomasini, Biaggini, Bassi, Fiscalini, Filipponi, Muscio, Maggoria, Storni, and Tognazzi began to appear along the north coast. This was a second or third stop in the pattern of immigration for many of the Italian Swiss. Many young men had come to work in dairying for older brothers in Marin and Sonoma counties. They were extremely independent, hard working, and thrifty. They came to the Central Coast to start out on their own.

Joseph Fiscalini arrived from Switzerland in 1876. His knowledge of the English language

Above: William Leffingwell, Sr., established one of the first sawmills in the Cambria area in 1863. He also built Leffingwell's Wharf about six miles south of San Simeon for lumber shipments. This photo dates from circa 1885. Courtesy, San Luis Obispo County Historical Museum

Right: These Chinese men were carrying a roast pig for a New Year's celebration around 1910. The Chinese established a presence in the Cambria area as laborers in the quicksilver mines. They were later involved in seaweed harvesting and established a Chinese Center in Cambria on Bridge Street south of Center. Dried seaweed and abalone were important shipments from Hearst's Wharf. Courtesy, San Luis Obispo County Historical Museum

was limited to a few necessary words. George Tognazzi had been here a bit longer. He knew enough English to help his fellow countryman get a job with Morgan Brians' large dairy operation in Green Valley.

Within two years Fiscalini had saved enough to go into partnership with John Filipponi. The two men leased property from George Hearst in Green Val-

ley and purchased 60 cows. By the end of the year they had made a $1,000 profit.

Lack of year-round transportation was the most limiting factor for the north coast. Captain John Wilson had developed the old landing once used by the priests from Mission San Miguel to ship their hides from San Simeon. Unfortunately, there were no good roads leading from the surrounding areas. William Leffingwell, Sr., arrived in the county in 1858 and established a landing four miles to the south. It was closer than Wilson's landing to the trails that came up from Morro down San Si-

meon Creek, where a number of American settlers were located. Leffingwell Landing briefly supplanted San Simeon as the principal harbor of the north coast.

Mining cinnabar became an important north coast activity during the Civil War. The ore, which produces mercury when heated in a retort, was discovered by a group of Mexicans in the Santa Lucia Range just east of San Simeon in 1862. It soon became apparent that the Franciscan Layer—the geologic layer of sandstone that ran the entire length of the Santa Lucias—bore rich cinnabar deposits.

Mercury was important to the federal government's prosecution of the Civil War as it was used in the primers of the infantryman's rifle. It was also used to amalgamate silver—the process by which silver was separated from the ore in western Nevada's Comstock Lode. This silver paid much of the great expense of "Mr. Lincoln's War." Leffingwell's Landing, and a team-powered sawmill that he constructed alongside Santa Rosa Creek, became vital to the mining enterprise.

Leffingwell also discovered veins of coal in the Cambria district, but the coal has never proven commercially viable. Quicksilver, however, attracted hundreds of experienced miners to the district.

The presence of cinnabar was, without doubt, a major factor in George Hearst's decision to purchase some 30,000 acres of the Rancho Piedra Blanca in 1865. The Missouri-born Hearst

Romualdo Pacheco was the only Hispanic to serve as governor of California. His mother, Ramona Carrillo Pacheco, married Captain John Wilson in 1836. Pacheco served in many elected positions, including lieutenant governor, and became governor when his predecessor, Newton Booth, became a U.S. senator. Courtesy, San Luis Obispo County Historical Museum

had come to California during the Gold Rush. He made his real fortune by investing his gold earnings in Nevada's Comstock Lode.

Hearst's interest in the Central Coast may well have been piqued by Romualdo Pacheco, stepson of Captain John Wilson. Pacheco had been selected by the Union Party as California's state treasurer in 1863. In that capacity, he came into contact with Hearst's associates, James Ben Ali Haggin and Lloyd Tevis. He later married Tevis' daughter Mabel. The 1862-1864 drought had brought financial woes to Pacheco and his mother, Ramona Carrillo Pacheco Wilson. Wilson's interests in the Piedra Blanca were a drain on the family's resources, while Hearst's preoccupation with gaining potential mining properties was well known. Pacheco was, without doubt, instrumental in bringing about the sale of the largest portion of "Totoi" Pico's Piedra Blanca Rancho. Pico received practically nothing from the Hearst purchase; the bulk of the proceeds from the sale in 1865 went to pay debts and to settle the Wilson-Pacheco family interests.

George Hearst had a variety of neighbors in the San Simeon - region, like Captain Joseph Clark, who established a Portuguese shore-whaling operation at Point San Simeon in 1864.

Clark's surname is deceptive, suggesting English, Irish, or Scandinavian ancestry. In fact, Clark was from the Azores; he had left the impoverished islands as a cabin boy

aboard a Danish ship. He learned reading, writing, and bookkeeping from the ship's captain, whose surname was Clark. Taking the same name, Clark proceeded to make a career for himself as a manager and business organizer for fellow countrymen who lacked his newly acquired talents.

George Hearst generally had friendly relations with Captain Clark and his shore whalers, but he also wanted to maximize the potential of his holdings. In 1878 Hearst constructed a 1,000-foot wharf with a narrow-gauge, horse-drawn railroad to facilitate the loading and unloading of the coastal packet steamers. During the wharf's first year of operation, it shipped butter, tallow, beef hides, wheat, barley, oats, dried seaweed, and abalone from the Chinese harvesters along the remote coast, and 169 flasks of mercury from the cinnabar mining operations in the Santa Lucias. Mercury prices were down, so this was well below the production and shipping figures for 1866 through 1876.

Hearst also erected a 4,800-foot warehouse, reputed to be one of the finest along the Pacific Coast, at the base of his wharf. It still stands today, across from the Sebastian Store and adjacent to a second warehouse designed by Julia Morgan and erected by William Randolph Hearst for landing his antiques during the 1920s. The local dairy farmers were the primary users of George Hearst's wharf during the First World War.

War, Beans, Boom, and Influenza

The First World War brought new prosperity to the Central Coast, particularly southern San Luis Obispo and northern Santa Barbara counties.

The region's transportation grid was especially dense in the south county, which was served after 1901 by the narrow-gauge Pacific Coast Railway and the mainline Southern Pacific with its freight and passenger terminals at Oceano. In addition there were county roads and, after 1915, a state motorway.

The Pacific Coast Railway's very existence was threatened by the coming of the Southern Pacific in 1901. The Espee, however, was mainly interested in long-haul service, and so the produce and seed growers of south county communities continued to rely on the "PC."

The "Great War" placed enormous strains on the American economy. The major portion of the fighting took place in Western Europe's industrial and agricultural heartland, crippling Europe's industry and specialized agriculture. The fighting in the east—between Germany and Austria-Hungary on one side and Tsarist Russia on the other —cut off Europe's customary backup supply of cereals from the breadbasket of the Ukraine.

As a result, the United States literally had to feed and clothe a continent at war. And it did so at considerable profit to its businessmen and farmers as the prices of agricultural commodities and manufactured items soared worldwide.

In the days before refrigeration was common, dried navy beans provided the most versatile emergency food source. While Herbert Hoover made a name for himself as the director of the Belgian Relief operation, the farmers of the Central

The Arroyo Grande Valley, seen here circa 1910, was barred from entering its produce in national competitions. This prompted the *Herald Recorder*, Arroyo's newspaper, to advertise on its masthead, "The only valley in the world that by reason of its prolific soil is barred from the National Seed Contests." Courtesy, San Luis Obispo County Historical Museum, Paulding Collection

Coast raised millions of pounds of beans for export.

Virtually all of the Pacific Coast Railway warehouses added bean-cleaning towers. These devices sifted off dirt and stones from the picked beans through a series of sieves. The price of cleaned navy beans, which was subsidized under war emergency measures, rose from 11½ cents to nearly 30 cents a pound. Previously untilled pastureland was quickly turned to bean production. San Luis Obispo and northern Santa Barbara counties literally kept the nation alive with their first-grade cleaned navy beans.

The fields just beyond the San Luis Obispo lighthouse at Point Buchon, along with patches of open land among the eucalyptus groves of the Nipomo Mesa, were quickly filled in with bean fields. Farmers could reap as much as $10,000-$15,000 a crop, with several crops a year.

The war also brought soldiers to San Luis Obispo for the first time since John C. Fremont's California Battalion of Mounted Infantry left in December 1846. The Union Oil Company's tank farm operation, just south of San Luis Obispo, and the Union Oil Wharf at Port San Luis were considered strategic resources, and so three companies of infantrymen were sent down from Fort Ord.

The prosperity was not without pain. After America's entry into the war in April 1917, a number of local boys went off to serve. The late Don McMillan of Shandon recalled the effect of going to France upon young men who had never spent much time beyond the Central Coast. The song "How Are You Gonna to Keep Them Down on the Farm after They've Seen Paaree?" was an apt expression of rural America's anxieties.

The last months of the war brought the Spanish influenza epidemic to the United States. The virus, so named because businessmen returning from Spain brought it to Paris and London, quickly spread among the millions of troops. In an era before antibiotics and sulfa drugs, the virus was a vicious killer. By the autumn of 1918 Stover Sanitarium, Pacific Hospital, Dr. Dower's Sanitarium in Oceano, and all other county facilities were overcrowded with seriously pneumonic patients. Schools were closed, and people wore face masks soaked in an astringent solution available at the Peoples Pharmacy, the Eagle Drugstore, and the Crocker Department Store. More than 30 adults and a number of children died in the epidemic.

The end of the war marked an end of government subsidies. It had been too good to last. The prudent grower had carefully sequestered his profits, but many others, like Atascadero's E.G. Lewis, were caught in the sudden drop as all government food contracts were cancelled.

The wartime profits had sparked a momentary boom, but expansion had to be handled carefully.

Top: Captain James Cass founded his business at present-day Cayucos in 1867. By 1875, with the financial backing of William Beebe, John Harford, and L. Schwartz, a town began growing up around Cass' wharf. Cass lived to see Cayucos grow before he died at the age of 92 in 1917. Courtesy, San Luis Obispo County Historical Museum

Bottom: By 1883, a few years before this photo was taken, Cambria was the second-largest city in the county, next to San Luis Obispo. A cinnabar rush in the 1870s spurred the town's growth. Courtesy, San Luis Obispo County Historical Museum

In the meantime, the town of Santa Rosa changed its name to Cambria, the Roman name for Wales. It generally is believed that the discovery of coal in the vicinity prompted Cambria's founders, George Lingo and P.A. Forrester, to give the town its new name, although it never proved profitable to mine.

The wharf at Cayucos was the product of the vision of an English sea captain and an American real-estate promoter: Captain James Cass and Chauncey Hatch Phillips, respectively.

Cass came to Cayucos in 1867. He claimed 360 acres of government land, but quickly lost interest in farming. With an eye to the sea, he started a lightering business, employing surf vessels to transport goods to and from the coastal steamers. Then, in partnership with Captain John Ingalls, he constructed a 380-foot wharf. The wharf, however, did not extend far enough out to anchor coastal shipping, so Cass then entered into a partnership with John Harford, William Beebe, and L. Schwartz, all of whom had been involved in the wharfage business at Avila and Port Harford (Port San Luis). The group, operating under the name of J. Cass and Co., spent over $15,000 in enlarging their operations. Cass constructed a spacious warehouse which housed the offices of the steamship and telegraph companies. He also built his own home, which still stands near the foot of the present county wharf in Cayucos.

Chauncey Hatch Phillips entered the scene just when the new wharf was completed in 1874. The state was in an economic slump. Land was cheap as a result, and Phillips saw the potential for development. This was his first real-estate promotion in the county. Phillips was instrumental in selling numerous dairy farms to the recently arrived Italian Swiss. In time, Cayucos came to be known as Little Italy because Italian was the principal language spoken on its streets.

The town of Morro Bay did not reach its potential until the Second World War, when the United States Navy dredged the harbor for a training base. Formed out of the Rancho Morro y Cayucos, the town of El Morro began in the 1860s. Ezra Stocking opened a store and post office in 1870, and a wharf was constructed in 1873. Unfortunately, several wrecks and near-misses scared the shipping companies away. Because of infrequent visits from the coastal steamers, Morro's population remained insignificant.

The rich dairy lands did provide incentives for road building, and the first county road was constructed from San Luis Obispo to San Simeon in 1870. This was followed by the construction of a county road over the Cuesta in 1876-1877. Both roads were built with the use

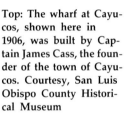

Top: The wharf at Cayucos, shown here in 1906, was built by Captain James Cass, the founder of the town of Cayucos. Courtesy, San Luis Obispo County Historical Museum

Bottom: The town of Cayucos, shown here in the early 1900s, takes its name from the small canoes sighted by the Portola expedition in 1769. It was founded by James Cass who built a wharf and began his shipping business there in 1867. Captain Cass' home still stands today on the main street of town. Courtesy, San Luis Obispo County Historical Museum

Left: James Blackburn, with his brother Daniel and brother-in-law Drury James, developed the Paso Robles Hot Springs, which became the city of Paso Robles. By 1864 a correspondent of the *San Francisco Bulletin* noted the springs as "the only place since we left San Jose where there appeared to be any life." Courtesy, San Luis Obispo County Historical Museum

Right: In the early 1880s the Hotel El Paso de Robles was photographed as the second hotel building was being built (in the background). The original hotel—built by the Blackburn brothers and their brother-in-law, Drury James, in 1864—marks the beginning of Paso Robles. Courtesy, San Luis Obispo County Historical Museum

of Chinese labor crews provided by Ah Louis. Ah Louis had formed an association with Harford, Beebe, and Schwartz as early as 1868. By 1877 the entire north-south axis of the county was linked by roads, connecting the dairy ranches of the coast with the county seat. San Luis Obispo, in turn, was linked to the wheat and cattle ranches of the north and south counties. The Pacific Coast Railway came through Arroyo Grande, Los Berros, and Nipomo before continuing on to Central City (Santa Maria), Los Alamos, and Los Olivos in northern Santa Barbara County, providing good access to sea transport at Port Harford. The railroad served as the keystone for bean production, which brought great prosperity to the county during the First World War, and the vegetable production for which the south county has been known ever since.

The Southern Pacific Railroad didn't reach the county until the autumn of 1886. The news that the Espee's Coast Route was going to run as far

south as San Miguel took many San Luis Obispo County ranchers and businessmen by surprise. For 13 years the railhead had been at Soledad, but in May 1886, the *San Luis Obispo Tribune* announced that 1,500 Chinese laborers were extending the line to the King Ranch. This ranch later became the town of King, now known as King City. On October 18, 1886, the first locomotive pulled into San Miguel.

It became apparent, however, that the railroad had no intention of stopping at the Old Mission settlement. Railroad crews could be heard blasting and laying down roadbed south of San Miguel even before the line from the north was completed.

The cattle ranchers of the north county had been waiting for this moment for years, and so the town of Paso Robles arose as the first "planned" city in the north. The town had its beginnings as a health spa; a mission vista, or *assistencia,* had been constructed south of the hot baths.

This large adobe structure was later occupied by Pedro Narvaez, the grantee of the Paso Robles rancho. Narvaez sold his interests to Petronilo Rios, who in 1857 sold out to James H. and Daniel Blackburn and their partner, Lazare Godchaux. Some evidence suggests that Rios thought he was merely leasing the land to the men, because the purchase price was a mere $8,000 for all 25,993 acres. The assessed value of the land was $29,900.

The partners divided the land three ways. Daniel Blackburn took the square league surrounding the hot springs. In 1865 he sold a half-interest in this to a Mr. McCreel, who almost immediately sold his portion to Drury James, Daniel Blackburn's brother-in-law and uncle to the famed outlaws, Jesse and Frank James. J.H. Blackburn bought back into a partnership that became known as Blackburn and James. The rest of the rancho remained in the hands of J.H. Blackburn and Godchaux.

Blackburn and James proceeded to develop the hot springs as a health spa. In 1864 German-born traveler and artist Edward Vischer visited the springs and observed that the mud baths' "medical virtues are even superior to water baths." By 1882 Blackburn and James had plans for an elaborate hotel on a site a mile and a half south of the springs. Waters and heated mud were brought to a bathhouse at the resort so that guests would not have to travel far from the comfort of

their rooms. A general store, post office, telegraph office, and Wells Fargo office were also located at the resort. The latter was operated by P.H. "Patsy" Dunn, brother-in-law to both Daniel Blackburn and Drury James.

When the railroad arrived in Paso Robles, Blackburn and James hired F.P. McCray of Hollister to lay out a townsite surround-

ing the resort. The plan was completed by G.F. Spurrier and Van R. Elliot in 1887. A newspaper, the *Paso Robles Leader*, was established in late 1886. Land sale promotions were held, for which Blackburn and James hired a brass band. A.R. Booth opened his Eagle Pharmacy in November 1886, after having opened a similar pharmacy in San Luis Obispo in partnership with B.G. Latimer.

The plan included a city

Paso Robles was a popular tourist location as early as the 1860s because of the healing properties of the hot springs and mud baths. With the coming of the railroad in the early 1880s, the town began to grow. Courtesy, San Luis Obispo County Historical Museum

Right: In 1908 the U.S. army held maneuvers in Paso Robles. This view shows machine gun practice with the Paso Robles bathhouse in the background. This bathhouse was built in 1888 and burned in 1913. The bivouac for the exercises was on the Atascadero Ranch, which later became the city of Atascadero. Courtesy, San Luis Obispo County Historical Museum

Above: Ignace Jan Paderewski was one of the most famous visitors to the Paso Robles area in the early-twentieth century. He eventually bought a ranch he called the Rancho San Ignacio outside the city. After World War I he returned to his native Poland to become the new country's president and did not return to Paso Robles. Courtesy, San Luis Obispo County Historical Museum

park at the center of town, on two square blocks donated by Blackburn and James. The beautifully planned town grew rapidly, having a second drugstore within a year.

In 1888 a new bathhouse was erected over the sulfur springs. The next year work was begun on the magnificent Hot Springs Hotel, although a slowdown in the economy prevented its completion until 1900. Nonetheless, the hotel attracted the rich and famous, such as Comstock Lode banker James Ralston; "Fighting Bob" Evans, the naval hero of the Spanish-American War; Governor Seymour of Oregon; and the Polish expatriate pianist, Ignacy Paderewski. The latter arrived with his hands badly crippled by arthritis. Within three months he was able to resume his concert tour.

A group of 12 businessmen in Paso Robles noted that access to the sulfur springs' curative powers had been limited to hotel residents. They petitioned and won the right to

drill for a sulfur spring on a site adjacent to the municipal park. William H. Weeks, the Watsonville architect who later designed the Carnegie libraries in Paso Robles and San Luis Obispo (as well as throughout Northern California) was hired to build a public bathhouse. Thereafter, local residents could enjoy mud baths for a mere 25 cents. Later, the public baths were offered to the city of Paso Robles and renamed the Municipal Bath House.

Meanwhile, the "Espee" traveled south to the townsite of Crocker, which had been laid out by the West Coast Land Company. A quarter section of land had been divided into lots of 100 by 150 feet, with larger "villa lots" of 5 to 10 acres on the town periphery. The land company also offered ranchos of 40 to 4,000 acres in the adjoining countryside.

The town was named in honor of Charles Crocker, a member of the "Big Four"—the men most closely involved in the actual building of the Southern Pacific (the other three men were Mark Hopkins, Collis P. Huntington, and Leland Stanford).

Crocker was most noted for initiating the policy of importing Chinese laborers to work on the railroad. In financial circles, however, he was better known for his real-estate developments, which he tied very closely to the routing of rail construction. He had recently developed the Del Monte Estates on the Monterey Peninsula, after constructing the "Del Monte Special" line to the site of his luxurious hotel and villas.

Crocker's land speculations often involved a great deal more risk than the Del Monte development. The company originally had been known as the Central Pacific and as such had earned an unenviable reputation. In 1870 the Big Four had purchased Timothy Phelps' Southern Pacific Railroad to build a San Francisco-San Diego line. They merged the Central Pacific with the Southern Pacific and, in 1873, dropped the original name of the trans-Sierra railroad entirely.

On March 17, 1884, the Big Four formed a new corporation in the state of Kentucky. None of their rails ran to that state, but Kentucky offered generous terms of incorporation—including limited liability for stockholders and the right to increase shares for whatever purpose without notifying the state. This allowed their operations a great deal of secrecy, which included becoming the silent partner in landholding companies.

The West Coast Land Company had been put together by Chauncey Hatch Phillips, who had come to California in 1864. He settled in Napa where he studied law and served as a dep-

Top: Captain Haley, a veteran of the Civil War, began the *Templeton Times* in 1886. The *Times* was funded by the West Coast Land Company, which was promoting Templeton. Haley later started a newspaper in Santa Margarita. Courtesy, San Luis Obispo County Historical Museum

Bottom: Templeton, shown here at the turn of the century, began as "Crocker" in 1886, named for Charles Crocker of the Southern Pacific. The name was changed to Templeton before the West Coast Land Company, which promoted the town, offered the land for sale. The West Coast Land Company was founded by Chauncey Hatch Phillips, with John Howard, R.E. Jack, and Isaac Goldtree. Courtesy, San Luis Obispo County Historical Museum

San Miguel was thriving as a railhead during the late 1880s and 1890s. The men in this photograph are (from left to right) Charles Forbes, Joe Riordan, L.R. Courter, an unidentified gentleman, Herman Rice, Wilkie Courter, and D.F. Mahoney. Courtesy, San Luis Obispo County Historical Museum

uty county clerk. He also became deputy collector of internal revenue for the federal government. For the next six years he served in the latter position, which didn't prevent him from working for the large mercantile banking firm of J.H. Goodman and Company. In 1871 he came to San Luis Obispo County and opened a bank with Horatio M. Warden, a Los Osos Valley rancher who later constructed two of the largest buildings in San Luis Obispo's downtown business district. The Bank of Warden and Phillips was later merged into the Bank of San Luis Obispo. It was so well managed that it re-

mained open when the Panic of 1875 ruined William Chapman Ralston's giant Bank of California—resulting in Ralston's suicide—and closed virtually every other bank in the state.

In 1878 Phillips retired from banking and went into real estate with Captain Cass at the Rancho Morro y Cayucos. He also promoted the Phillips Addition, a subdivision just off Palm Street in northern San Luis Obispo, as well as land on the Corral de Piedra, Arroyo Grande, and Pismo ranches. His largest early development was at the Huer-Huero Rancho where he laid out the town of

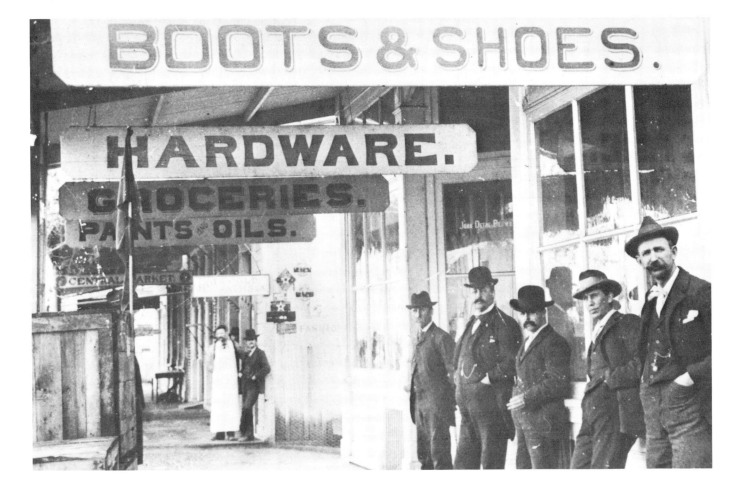

Creston, offering ranches for as little as $20 an acre. He also promoted land sales along the Pacific Coast Railroad's right-of-way at the towns of Los Alamos and Los Olivos in northern Santa Barbara County.

He was instrumental in organizing the West Coast Land Company in 1886. John Howard served as president; R.E. Jack, co-owner of the huge Rancho Cholame and related by marriage to Colonel W.W. Hollister, was treasurer; and long-time San Luis Obispo businessman Isaac Goldtree was vice president. But it clearly was Phillips who ran the show locally, and the town of Crocker was to be, perhaps, his greatest achievement.

Phillips let it be known that he had 5,000 sets of maps and an equal number of catalogues for the promotion. He announced that 1,500 initial mailings had been prepared, but before they could be sent, the town changed its name to Templeton. The name usually is associated with the youngest of Charles Crocker's three sons, though this fact was never formally announced. Quite possibly Phillips feared that the slow pace of early town-lot sales—the country ranches sold well—reflected a popular distrust of Crocker and the Espee.

Crocker had already begun a game of hardball with the business community in the county seat of San Luis Obispo. The railroad was scheduled to turn west toward Morro Bay, following the route later taken by State Highway 41. References had appeared in the *San Luis*

Obispo Tribune suggesting that "Crocker, being the last town before ascending the grade to Morro Bay, will very likely have machine shops and workshops of the Southern Pacific Railroad."

Rumors circulated that Crocker and the railroad planned to bypass San Luis Obispo entirely by running a route through Morro Bay, the Los Osos Valley, and Pismo Beach. Charlie Crocker's name,

In 1888 Santa Margarita was laid out on Patrick Murphy's ranch. It boomed as the Southern Pacific's railhead for five years, from 1889-1894, while the railroad was built across the Cuesta. Santa Margarita's main street is seen here circa 1910. Courtesy, San Luis Obispo County Historical Museum

as a result, would not have been popular with many San Luis Obispans. The feeling that Crocker and the Espee were behind the West Coast Land Company was reinforced by the name of the town. And so the name was changed.

Phillips touted the fine education available at the Templeton Institute, a privately financed educational facility that would take students from the primary grades through college. It also of-

Top: Atascadero, founded by E.G. Lewis in 1914, boasted a major rotogravure printing plant. This plant printed the rotogravure sections for Los Angeles and San Francisco-area newspapers, which were shipped by rail from Atascadero to the respective newspapers. This building is still in use today as a masonic hall. Courtesy, San Luis Obispo County Historical Museum

Bottom: The Stenner Creek Trestle was built by the Southern Pacific in 1894. The trestle's crossing of Stenner Creek was considered an engineering marvel. It was barely completed in time for the scheduled first run (San Francisco to San Luis Obispo) on May 5, 1894. Courtesy, San Luis Obispo County Historical Museum

fered courses up through the secondary level, under the guidance of its director, Professor J.D.E. Summers. Tuition ranged from $12.50 to $25 a term.

But not even the offer of high-quality private schooling was a sufficient attraction. Finally Phillips announced that he and his wife, who were the parents of the wife of the English novelist Horace Ainsley Vachell, were moving from San Luis Obispo to Templeton. Today their home has been nicely restored as a "bed and breakfast" establishment on Templeton's main street.

The mainline Southern Pacific made boomtowns out of San Miguel and Paso Robles, but before the railroad could reach San Luis Obispo or Morro Bay, an economic downturn took place. The 1890s were not a happy time in the United States. The Panic of 1893 had frozen investment capital, and the Southern California land boom of the 1880s had resulted in a great deal of overspeculation. The fortunes of large corporations and great families soured. The Espee reached as

far as Santa Margarita by 1889, but went no further for six years.

A townsite was surveyed in 1889, and Santa Margarita became the lively headquarters for the work crews preparing the tunnels across the southern limit of the Santa Lucia Range.

Meanwhile, Johann Henrik, Baron von Schroeder, a retired Prussian Army officer, purchased land at the northeastern base of the Santa Lucias, just northwest of Santa Margarita. He erected a beautifully landscaped home for himself, calling it the Eagle Ranch. The baron brought notoriety to the county in the late 1890s when he was accused of attempting to seduce young girls at parties

in San Francisco and Marin counties. He returned to Germany to fight for the Fatherland in August 1914, and his land was seized by the federal government under the Alien Property Act in May 1917.

East of the Eagle Ranch was the Henry Ranch, where the Southern Pacific maintained a flag stop used by farmers from the Creston district. The stop's name changed from the Spanish *Paloma* to the English "Dove," and finally to the less peaceable "Eaglet" in honor of the von Schroeder ranch. The 23,000-acre Henry Ranch was purchased by E.G. Lewis in 1913 and became Atascadero Colony, now the city of Atascadero.

Meanwhile, by 1892, new energies and business attractions had sparked the Espee's passage across the Santa Lucias. Seven tunnels were bored through the ridge on the west side of Cuesta Canyon. An elaborate trestle had to be constructed over Stenner Creek, where the tracks descended from the southern grade workstations at Goldtree and Serrano.

The first train was scheduled to come down the grade on Saturday, May 5, 1894. The town was overtaken by excitement over the completion of San Luis Obispo's first rail link to the outside world. A committee was formed to celebrate the event, and a giant barbecue serving $330 worth of meat and food was planned. The grandest of the town's hotels, the 144-room Ramona Hotel, had been completed in 1888, anticipating the arrival of the railroad. Now it was filled with ranchers and their families from throughout the Central Coast, all anticipating the historic moment.

The three horse-drawn streetcars connecting the Ramona Hotel at the northern end of San Luis Obispo with the narrow-gauge Pacific Coast Railway depot at South and Higuera streets were kept on a busy schedule, with a single horse often pulling cars overflowing with more than 20 adults.

The Pacific Coast line would still be the link to the sea at Port San Luis and to the south county communities of Pismo, Arroyo Grande, Grover City, Los Berros, and Nipomo, as well as Santa Maria, Orcutt, Los Alamos, and Los Olivos in Santa Barbara County.

Benjamin Brooks, editor of the *Morning Tribune*, kept a close eye on the project. In late April he went out to Stenner Creek Road at the base of the grade, where contractor Tommy Thompson was constructing the trestle. Thompson, amused at the queries of the newspaperman, who apparently knew very little about metal fabrication, told the editor, "I have contracted to complete the bridge in 12 days, but I do not believe it can be done." Brooks bought the deception, and on May 1 reported that he thought it impossible that the rail would stretch the 10,000

Top: This rare view shows a captive balloon hovering over the grounds of the Ramona Hotel in the late 1890s. Events such as these were staged for entertainment by itinerant balloonists throughout the country, who in some cases made extra money on the side by photographing bird's-eye-views of the communities below. Courtesy, San Luis Obispo County Historical Museum

Bottom: A barbecue was held on the grounds of the Ramona Hotel on May 5, 1894. This big event marked the coming of the Southern Pacific to San Luis Obispo, and was part of the festivities which occurred throughout the community. It was on this site that the Ramona Depot, now preserved by the San Luis Obispo County Historical Society, was later built. Courtesy, San Luis Obispo County Historical Museum

Top: The San Luis Street Railway was a horse-drawn car which ran on rails laid in Higuera Street. Built with Chinese labor, it first ran on October 14, 1887. The car stopped running in 1905 after its terminus, the Ramona Hotel, burned. Courtesy, San Luis Obispo County Historical Museum

Bottom: This view shows the paving of Bridge Street in Arroyo Grande at the turn of the century. With the coming of the Pacific Coast Railway, Arroyo Grande had become a railhead for a vast agricultural district. With the ensuing growth, roads were constantly being upgraded and improved. Courtesy, San Luis Obispo County Historical Museum

yards from the grade to the depot by May 5.

In fact, the rail link was completed—but not properly —on May 5, 1894. The contractors, working under incredible pressure, laid down only every other tie along the roadbed, which itself was not filled in with ballast nor graveled. The work of laying the last three miles of track continued up through Friday morning, May 4. Finally the track reached the edge of the Ramona Hotel,

where the Ramona Depot stood (between Marsh and Higuera at Johnson, across from the present-day Vons Supermarket. Essex Street, the other cross-street, has long since vanished).

At 3:35 p.m., a light engine from a work train glided down the grade, over the trestle at Stenner Creek Road, which still had many bolts missing, and came to a stop at the railway entrance to the Ramona Hotel. The engineer blew the whistle of the locomotive in triumph. The enormous siren at the Pacific Coast Railyard, over a mile to the south, responded with its deep howl.

Bells sounded from the mission, from St. Stephen's Episcopal Church, and from the firehouse at city hall on Higuera Street. The steam whistle at the gas and electrical works at Pismo and Archer, adjacent to the Pacific Coast Lumber Yard, let off a mighty blast. San Luis Obispo's days of isolation were

ended. The arrival of the first passenger train the next day was almost anticlimactic. The Middle Kingdom had come of age.

San Luis Obispo's rail link was only to the north. The link to Los Angeles remained stalled at Ellwood Station near Goleta until 1900. Then, with a characteristic spurt of energy, the mighty Espee began building again. The major obstacles included the trestles across stormy creeks at Gaviota and the bridge across the Santa Ynez River at Surf. The connection with the south was finally made in March 1901. Passengers en route to Los Angeles were obliged to travel inland along the Santa Clara River on the southern edge of Ventura, proceeding by way of Saugus Junction on into Los Angeles—via the same San

Top: With the coming of the Southern Pacific in 1894, businesses designed to serve the railroaders grew up around the SP yards. The Glen Dell Hotel, later renamed the Park Hotel and recently renovated by the City of San Luis Obispo, catered to SP employees and travelers. Courtesy, San Luis Obispo County Historical Museum

Bottom: A photograph was taken of the corner of Monterey and Court streets in San Luis Obispo around 1890. The building housing the Loobliner store has served in many capacities through the years, including the post office, and today is a restaurant. On the site of the bank across Court Street was the Casa Grande of Captain Dana, which leased space for the first courthouse of the county. Courtesy, San Luis Obispo County Historical Museum

Top: Richard Nixon, during his campaign for president in 1960, stopped in San Luis Obispo and spoke from the steps of the county courthouse. Courtesy, San Luis Obispo County Historical Museum

Bottom: The Bello Street Bridge in Pismo Beach, abandoned today, was built for Highway 2, which later became Highway 101. It is one of only four bridges left from this first California state coastal highway. Courtesy, Mark P. Hall-Patton

Fernando-Burbank-Glendale route employed by the San Joaquin Valley trains. A train carrying President William McKinley —the first of many famous leaders to travel through the Middle Kingdom—took the Coast Route through San Luis Obispo in March 1901.

Perhaps the most exceptional of all visiting politicians was Soviet Premier Nikita S. Khrushchev, who came through San Luis Obispo aboard the Espee Daylight during the late summer of 1959. The Daylight's route took Khrushchev directly through the still-under-construction Vandenberg Air Force Base, where, along with giant rocket gantries, the Soviet leader could not help but observe the Air Force greeting along the tracks: "Peace is our Mission."

Five years later, the first state highway bond act was passed, and California Motorway Number 2 reached San Luis Obispo. The El Camino Real thus began the long process of taking on its now familiar freeway form. Leaving the San Luis Obispo Mission from the plaza side of the "L", coming out past the "fish pond" that is singularly lacking in goldfish, and taking the steps down to Chorro Street, one will encounter a sign hanging from a tall shepherd's staff. This is one of the few remaining highway signs for the old State Highway 2, the El Camino Real that became Highway 101. The sign was erected, in an era of minimal government, by the San Luis Obispo Parlor of the Native Daughters of the Golden West. The bond act did not provide sufficient funds for directional signs, so the private sector—led by the Automobile Club of Southern California, the Native Daughters, and later, an alliance of Coast Route chambers of commerce called the Mission Trails Association—did the job with style.

Top: Because of transportation improvements, by the 1950s Avila had increased its popularity as a summer retreat from the heat. This view of the beach dates from circa 1955. The Avila school can be seen on the hill to the right in the trees. Courtesy, San Luis Obispo County Historical Museum

Bottom: Beachfront communities such as Pismo Beach have grown since 1945 with vacationers seeking cooling days along the coast. The widening of Highway 101 during the 1950s to four lanes has helped to accommodate the visitors. Courtesy, San Luis Obispo County Historical Museum

Stories of the Depression

Stanley Willard worked for George Lewis on his Carrizo Plains ranch when he first arrived in San Luis Obispo County in 1932. Like many new-comers to the county, jobs were hard to come by, and though he had no experience with a Cat-erpillar, he ran it when asked. Courtesy, Eleanor and Pat Brown

Facing page bottom: J.J. Andre was noted for his generosity during the worst days of the Depres-sion. In this view of his store, taken around 1915, the variety of merchan-dise he carried is shown. The men in the photo-graph are from left to right, Manual T. Avila, two unknown gentle-men, Tony Escobar, and Joe Reis. Courtesy, San Luis Obispo County Historical Museum

During the early 1900s, San Luis Obispo had a fairly well-balanced economy. Its dairy-ing and cattle industries had suf-fered greatly from the epidemic of hoof and mouth disease during the early 1920s; hence the region did not contract exces-sive debt. Initially, it did not suffer as badly as other regions during the onset of the Great Depression. People still had to eat, and while dairying, truck farming, and beef industries en-dured losses in profit, produc-tion levels were maintained.

Unemployed agricultural workers, often once farm owners themselves, flocked to the region. Eleanor Willard Brown recalls how her family came west from North Dakota in the tormented Dust Bowl in 1932. Her father, Stanley Wil-lard, obtained work on the George Lewis Carrizo Plains ranch. Eleanor remembers that "it was time to prepare the spring crop. Dad was a little

apprehensive about running a Caterpillar because the truth was that he was only experi-enced in running a tractor."

Later in the Depression, famed photographer Dorothea Lange took her well known "Migrant Mother" photo of Flor-ence Thompson, an Oklahoma Dust Bowl immigrant who had come to Nipomo hoping to find work picking peas. She found that all the jobs were taken by immigrant Filipino laborers. She allegedly sold the wheels off her beaten-up automobile, her only means of transportation, in order to purchase milk and food for her children. This became one of the most symbolic images of the Great Depression in America.

The Depression had another side, one of cooperation and trust among old friends. Attor-ney Peter Andre recalls how his father, J.J. Andre, had ex-tended credit limits at his An-dre Grocery. J.J. kept many of

Top: In 1936 Farm Security Administration photographer Dorthea Lange was taking photographs in a pea-pickers' camp on the Nipomo Mesa. As she was leaving, she saw Florence Thompson, a migrant laborer and widow with six children. Lange did not ask Thompson's name, but did record her age and took six pictures of Thompson. This image, known as "Migrant Mother," became one of the most famous visual records of the Depression. Courtesy National Archives

the Portuguese families in the county, especially the residents of the Irish Hills west of the Los Osos Valley, alive during the worst years of the Depression. Finally, J.J. reached his own credit limit with the bank. Hundreds of families were depending on him, yet he couldn't obtain funds to restock his shelves.

J.J. went to fellow grocer and then-mayor Louis Sinsheimer. He asked Sinsheimer, the most prosperous merchant in San Luis Obispo, for a $10,000 loan until the harvest came in and the farmers could pay on their debts. Sinsheimer quickly agreed to the loan. J.J. asked how the papers should be drawn up. Sinsheimer said, "That's not necessary—a handshake will suffice."

6 San Luis Obispo and the Cal Poly Tradition

Mrs. Halte taught at the Huasna School around 1890. The establishment of a school district was often seen as the first major sign of civilization in sparsely populated rural areas. The upper Arroyo Grande Valley experienced a great deal of growth during this period through the coming of the Pacific Coast Railway. Courtesy, San Luis Obispo County Historical Museum

The world beyond the Middle Kingdom associates San Luis Obispo County with three well-known institutions: William Randolph Hearst's *La Cuesta Encantada* above San Simeon Bay, more commonly known as Hearst Castle; Alex and Phyllis Madonna's elegant hostelry, Madonna Inn; and California Polytechnic State University. The first two attract tourists, many of whom return as often as possible. The latter has become a greatly sought-after public institution of higher education. Because of space limitations, it can admit only one out of five qualified applicants. Over Cal Poly's 87-year history its graduates have made numerous contributions to the arts and sciences, and to the United States of America. Several thousand of its graduates have either remained in San Luis Obispo County, or returned after a career elsewhere to make major contributions to life on the Central Coast.

The Cal Poly tradition is the product of the pragmatism of the American West. The men who conceived of and fought for the school, like the state and town that gave it birth, were enmeshed in the irrepressible

The main house of William Randolph Hearst's La Cuesta Encantada is shown here under construction in the 1920s. Hearst inherited great landholdings, acquired by his father George Hearst, after the death of his mother, Phoebe Apperson Hearst, in 1919. His "castle" was donated to the State of California after his death, and was opened to the public in 1958. Courtesy, San Luis Obispo County Historical Museum

optimism that characterized America's expansion westward during the second half of the nineteenth century.

Myron Angel, a well-known journalist and historian, was the individual most responsible for the founding of the polytechnic school. The course of Angel's life parallels the movement west.

Born in 1827 in Oneonta, New York, he spent his boyhood upstate. In later life, Angel recalled that he had witnessed the transitions from the Mohawk Trail of the colonial era to the Erie Canal constructed by the young republic, and from that to the building of the Hudson Valley Railroad.

Angel was granted an appointment to the United States Military Academy at West Point in 1846. In 1849 he dropped out, joining his brother Eugene in the trek to the goldfields of California. After months of travel, the last several hundred miles on foot along the Old Spanish Trail from Santa Fe, the Angel brothers reached San Diego. Their clothes were in tatters and they were barefoot, carrying all their belongings on their backs.

They spent their last remaining money on passage aboard a brig to San Francisco. Penniless, they could not rent lodgings. They spent their first night in the "Metropolis of the West," wandering along the mud-filled streets.

The next morning Myron was offered a job shingling a roof. Labor was scarce because of the attraction of the Mother

Lode. The wages were excellent, but Angel was forced to turn the job down. In his 1908 *History of the California Polytechnic School at San Luis Obispo,* he admitted that "I never drove a nail in my life."

Like most of the forty-niners, Angel had only indifferent luck finding gold. He turned to ranching in Colusa County, forming a significant tie to California's agricultural traditions.

During the 1860s Angel turned to journalism, becoming editor of newspapers in Placerville, Sacramento, and Oakland. While in Oakland, he formed an association with the Thompson and West Company. The latter were engaged in producing a series of histories of the towns and counties of the far west. Angel wrote the histories of several counties and communities, as well as the first history of the newly formed state of Nevada.

In 1883 Angel came to San Luis Obispo to write the first formal history of the county. He purchased a home in the city of San Luis Obispo, produced the history, then became the editor of the *Tribune* and later the *Republic,* the city's two leading newspapers. He also became

Mabel Lewis, William and Millicent Hearst, and E.G. Lewis stopped for a photograph on the steps of the Women's Magazine Building in University City, Missouri, in 1913. William Hearst and E.G. Lewis both had tremendous impact on the county during the twentieth century, between Hearst's La Cuesta Encantada and Lewis' Atascadero Colony. Courtesy, San Luis Obispo County Historical Museum

This late-1920s view of construction at William Randolph Hearst's La Cuesta Encantada was taken by J.J. Boyd, who worked at the castle. W.R. Hearst's "castle," as it is called today, was given to the State of California and opened as a State Park in 1958. Courtesy, San Luis Obispo County Historical Museum

the city's leading civic booster. He spent most of the remainder of his life in San Luis Obispo, dying there in 1911.

Angel was the principal activist in attracting the Southern Pacific Railroad's Coast Route into San Luis Obispo in 1894. The community's first permanent economic base came with the railroad shops and roundhouse that were necessitated by the railroad's ascent over the Santa Lucia Range via the Cuesta Pass tunnels.

As the Southern Pacific's arrival from the north became a certainty, Angel searched for other ways to assure San Luis Obispo's lasting stature among California communities. The 1890s were a period of economic consolidation. Californians were just beginning to recognize education as

Top: This engraving of Myron Angel appeared in the 1891 *A Memorial and Biographical History of the Counties of Santa Barbara, San Luis Obispo and Ventura, California,* by Yda Addis Storke. Angel wrote the first history of the county, and served as the editor of the *San Luis Obispo Tribune* and later the *San Luis Obispo Daily Republic.* His efforts were instrumental in the founding of Cal Poly. Courtesy, San Luis Obispo County Historical Museum

Bottom: Farmers throughout the county would benefit from the establishment of Cal Poly. This threshing crew worked for Alva Paul around 1905. Courtesy, San Luis Obispo County Historical Museum

forming part of a secure base for commerce and agriculture. The University of California had been chartered by the state legislature in 1868 and founded in Oakland the following year. The first state normal school (teacher training academy), the parent of the California State University System, was founded in San Francisco in 1857. It later became San Francisco State University. A small college was opened in San Jose in 1857, but did not attain normal school status until 1871. Los Angeles received a normal school in 1882, as did Chico in 1889.

In each case these schools gave their respective locales a more dignified status and respectability. They also benefited the commerce of the community as young ladies and gentlemen took up residence for teacher training and their families took notice of the locale.

In 1893 Angel made a visit to his birthplace in Oneonta. The once rough-and-tumble town on the western frontier of New York State had been transformed into a refined, urbane city. Angel was very much impressed by the changes and credited them to the influence of a local normal school. He resolved that this was exactly what San Luis Obispo needed.

When Angel returned to San Luis Obispo, he contacted the district's state senator, Sylvester C. Smith of Bakersfield. A statewide drought in the early 1890s had hurt state revenues and nothing could be accomplished until 1896.

On January 15, 1896, Senator Smith submitted a bill proposing a normal school for San Luis Obispo. Unfortunately, just a few days before, another bill had been submitted advocating a similar institution for San Diego. The legislature named a select committee to examine the prospects of each city. San Luis Obispo's chances did not appear good.

In the meantime, Senator Smith suggested an alternate proposal to Angel: "that the plan be changed to that for a polytechnic school." On February 3, 1897, Smith introduced a bill for that purpose.

The Felipe Moraga Adobe stood on land that is now part of Cal Poly. Courtesy, Southwest Museum, Guy Giffen Collection

On February 20, 1897, the select committee of the legislature arrived in San Luis Obispo after its visit to San Diego. The city council, in its eagerness to gain the normal school, appropriated $100 for a banquet and reception at the elegant 103-room Ramona Hotel. When Angel was summoned to give the final speech at the banquet, he surprised the audience with a dramatic shift in tactics. He had been the leading spokesperson for a normal school. In front of this prestigious group, he spoke effusively of a different sort of school: An institution that would "teach the hand as well as the head so that no young man or woman will be sent off in the world to earn their living as poorly equipped as I was when I landed in San Francisco in 1849."

The plans for the local normal school were put aside. In less than a month, the polytechnic school bill had passed both houses of the legislature with only a handful of dissenting votes. But in April 1897, Governor James H. Budd vetoed the bill on the grounds that such a school was not needed and would increase taxation.

In November 1900, Warren N. John of San Luis Obispo was elected to the legislature. This young, ambitious businessman joined with Senator Smith in ensuring the passage of the bill. They prevented a gubernatorial veto based on lack of funds by inserting a clause that no money for the institute would be made available until

January 1, 1902.

Local citizens launched a countywide campaign to guarantee passage of the bill and its signing by Governor Henry Gage. A statewide campaign by Angel, John, Smith, and *San Luis Obispo Tribune* editor Benjamin Brooks brought endorsements from influential leaders like Stanford University President David Starr Jordan. The key ingredient may well have been the Southern Pacific Railway, which only recently had closed the final gap in the Coast Route south to Los Angeles, from present-day Goleta to Surf at the mouth of the Santa Ynez River.

In February 1901 the act passed the Senate by a vote of 33 to 3 and the Assembly by a vote of 51 to 1. The following March 1, Governor Gage signed the act into law.

From the beginning the notion of teaching the hand as

Cal Poly's educational emphasis from its beginnings was on practical education. This is a view of the wood-shop around 1915. Courtesy, San Luis Obispo County Historical Museum

Facing page: Cal Poly began as a coeducational school. This view shows a home economics course circa 1915. It was not until 1929 that the school was open to men only, becoming coed again in 1956. Courtesy, San Luis Obispo County Historical Museum

well as the mind manifested itself as the Cal Poly style. The school's first director, Dr. Leroy Anderson, who served from 1902 to 1907, emphasized the school's mission—serving a state-wide base of students, learning by doing, and instituting Cal Poly's hands-on approach to its polytechnic subject matter.

Through the construction of a dormitory building, the school's tradition as a residence institution was firmly ensconced. The building was still littered with construction debris on October 1, 1903, the day that classes were first held. The power plant and heating facilities hadn't been started. But school began on time.

After Anderson's departure in 1908, the school began to evolve into the equivalent of a junior college. Governing responsibility was transferred from a local board of trustees to the State Board of Education. The First World War brought a higher proportion of women to the school, and during the 1920s the school served increasingly higher numbers of San Luis Obispo residents, who regarded it as an attractive alternative to the local high school and junior college. Partly because of this short-lived departure from serving a statewide base of students, California's fiscally conservative Governor Friend C. Richardson sought to close the school.

Benjamin Ray Crandall, director from 1924 to 1933, made valiant efforts to correct the changes, but when the Great Depression's impact was fully felt, the legislature threatened to abolish the school.

A new beginning came in 1933, when Julian A. McPhee, chief of the California Bureau of Agricultural Education, offered to become the school's president while retaining responsibility for the Bureau.

Contrary to a widely held view, President McPhee did not limit enrollment to men. This was done by Director Crandall in 1929. But McPhee did make many other changes in guiding Cal Poly into a new era. Operating at first on a bare-bones budget, McPhee restored Cal Poly to statewide prominence. He secured a solid financial backing for the institution, based on a share of the revenues derived by the state from the levy on pari-mutuel betting at licensed horse-racing facilities. A third year of instruction was added to the program in 1936, and a fourth year in 1940. The first baccalaureate degree exercises were held on May 28, 1942.

By that time the Second World War had transformed the campus. President McPhee contacted Secretary of the Navy Frank Knox and almost immediately received authorization to begin a Naval Flight Preparatory School on the campus. Wartime programs such as this, as well as the Academic Refresher Courses for military personnel, brought many young men into contact with the schools. A significant number of these men returned to the school on the G.I. Bill after the war.

The Second World War

The rural dairying, wheat, and truck farming county of San Luis Obispo went to war earlier than many other parts of the United States. Because of its proximity to the Pacific, its transportation connections to the Los Angeles Basin and the San Francisco Bay Area, its nearness to California's agricultural heartland, and its vast quantities of rugged landscape, the Central Coast was picked as a key military training area by the War Department.

As early as 1902, the Army Corps of Engineers had expressed an interest in acquiring the Nacimiento Ranch on the Monterey county line. By the spring of 1940, six ranches were leased for the purpose of constructing a training facility for 30,000 men. Construction started on November 15, 1940, although the ranches weren't actually purchased until 1943. Eventually, 8,000 workers were involved in building what became Camp Roberts. The camp's construction, and operation until the end of the war, revolutionized the economy of the rustic north county ranching community of San Miguel.

Camp Roberts officially began its training mission in March of 1941. At that time it was ranked as the world's largest military training facility—436,000 men went through the camp's 17-week cycles of intensive discipline and instruction.

Another major San Luis Obispo military outpost, Camp San Luis Obispo, began as a National Guard training facility in 1928. Located in the southwestern portion of the Chorro Valley, it became the summer headquarters for the California National Guard. Although activities were virtually suspended during the early years of the Depression, the Guard was revived in 1934 by California's new governor, Frank F. Merriam. Merriam had called up the Guard to suppress the San Francisco great strike of 1934. He made a strong issue of the National

Top: The civilian effort to win World War II included bond drives boasting patriotic slogans. These two examples, created by Young Louis, the eldest son of Ah Louis, are shown in the lobby of the Fremont Theater, where Louis was a projectionist. Courtesy, San Luis Obispo County Historical Museum

Bottom: This view of Camp Luis Obispo, taken in 1934, shows the tent encampment of the State National Guard. During World War II the camp blossomed into one of the major army training bases in the United States. Courtesy, San Luis Obispo County Historical Museum

Guard in the famous election between himself and Upton Sinclair. The Camp was briefly renamed Camp Merriam.

During the fall of 1940 the War Department began the process of leasing ranches adjacent to Camp Merriam. Construction began immediately, hampered by 36 inches of rain between January and March, 1941. While the Central Coast has had heavier rains since, especially in 1969, 1973, and 1983, drainage facilities were nonexistent in

1941. Whole portions of the camp were swamped and had to be rebuilt. Millions of dollars in construction equipment and material were lost. All this added tremendously to the bill for the camp: $17,000,000!

On August 14, 1941, the *Telegram-Tribune* ran a headline announcing: "U.S. SENATE GROUP ATTACKS CAMP ABOUT BUILDING COSTS." Senator Harry S. Truman's committee on wartime waste and mismanagement labeled Camp San Luis Obispo's construction costs "unduly and unnecessarily high." Only those who had actually endured the rains could understand why.

Morro Bay received a naval station; Paso Robles an army air corps landing field. Northern Santa Barbara County had a similar landing field at Captain Allen Hancock's airport south of Santa Maria. Camp Cook—later Vandenberg Air Force Base—was constructed as a rugged infantry training

Top: Santa Margarita Dam was built by the Army Corps of engineers in 1942 to supply water for Camp San Luis Obispo. This view shows the construction of the diversion ditch and bypass pipe. Through the efforts of then-Mayor Fred Kimball, San Luis Obispo also received water from this development. Courtesy, San Luis Obispo County Historical Museum

Bottom: The impact of 10,000 troops and nearly that many dependents put a strain on the county in 1942. This view shows some of the troops in formation on Monterey Street in front of Mission San Luis Obispo for Armed Services Day in 1943. The county worked together to accommodate the soldiers, many of whom returned to settle here after the war. Courtesy, San Luis Obispo County Historical Museum

facility on 100,000 acres northwest of Lompoc. Cal Poly trained some 3,600 aviation cadets in its Naval Flight Preparation School and some 1,100 servicemen in its Academic Refresher Unit.

Between the fall of 1941 and August 1945, more than 75,000 military personnel were stationed in the rural valleys of the Central Coast. Banks were overwhelmed on payday, and the lines outside public phones sometimes stretched for a block or more with anxious soldiers trying to call home. (The region didn't have dial tone phones for another two decades—you had to ring the operator.)

The wartime experience forever changed San Luis Obispo. The trainees liked what they saw in the region. Thousands came back—many to marry local girls; others to attend Cal Poly. Hundreds more retired along the Central Coast 30 and 40 years later.

Today dozens of Cal Poly students speak with pride of a grandfather who was at Camp Roberts or Camp San Luis during the Second World War.

The original effort to found Cal Poly was made by Myron Angel, a newspaperman and writer of the first history of the county. Through the efforts of Assemblyman Warren M. John and State Senator S.C. Smith, a bill to create a state "Polytechnic School" was introduced and passed in the 1900-1901 California legislative session. The first school building, shown here, was built in 1903. Courtesy, San Luis Obispo County Historical Museum

In the great postwar expansion, the school received a name change—from California State Polytechnic School to California State Polytechnic College. Some graduate-level programs were introduced into a widely expanded curriculum, and the return of coeds in 1956 began another alteration in campus life.

In 1961 the campus, under the State Master Plan for Higher Education, was brought into what is now the California State University System. It became California Polytechnic State University in the summer of 1972.

Programs continued to build, along with enrollment, under President McPhee, whose tenure in office witnessed an explosive growth—from 117 students in 1933, to 7,740 at the time of his retirement in 1966.

The new programs have included internationally recognized curricula in architecture, graphic arts, computer science, business, and international agriculture. All of these blossomed under the 12-year presidency of McPhee's successor, Robert E. Kennedy, and continue to grow under President Warren J. Baker.

The unique campus programs and attractive environment have made Cal Poly one of the most sought-after options among institutions of higher education throughout the United States. Visitors to the campus continually remark on its clean appearance. The Cal Poly students really care about this very special place. Perhaps that is the greatest legacy of the founders in instituting a holistic approach to education: bringing mind and body together, and educating the whole person.

Mission Restoration and Uncovered Secrets

T he railroad's arrival in San Luis Obispo County during the late 1800s was largely responsible for the boom of 1914-1919, when the Central Coast became the bean exporting capital of the world. The war left many farmers unbelievably rich. However, many of them lost their newfound wealth when the government abruptly cut off the magnificently high subsidized prices in December 1918. Hoof-and-mouth disease, a legacy of the trench warfare in Europe, also badly damaged the animal herds, making the 1920s a less than prosperous period.

The town was much in need of repair. The Old Mission was in terrible shape, so much so that it was nearly lost.

Mission San Luis Obispo resumed its life as a parish church during the 1850s. By that time virtually all of the native Chumash who possessed the skills for working with adobe had died of typhus. The few remaining were to die of cholera during the drought years of the mid-1860s. In the meantime the local population had removed many of the roof tiles for their

Mission San Luis Obispo was the only structure of any size in the area for many years, but by the late-nineteenth century, when this picture was taken, it was nearly a ruin in the middle of town. The mission was sided with wood in the 1880s, which had to be removed in the 1920s. The courtyard shown here also shows the falling down "Padre's Kitchen," which actually served as a storage building since 1800. Courtesy, San Luis Obispo County Historical Museum

Top: Mission San Luis Obispo was photographed here in the mid-1880s. Notice the New England-style bell-tower and the clapboard siding on part of the building. This is the period in which the church was sided, for protection, but the end of the building nearest the camera, and the columns, were allowed to deteriorate. The recently installed gaslight at the corner of Monterey and Broad streets shows how San Luis Obispo came of age in the 1880s. Courtesy, San Luis Obispo County Historical Museum

Bottom: Fire was a constant danger in communities built mainly of wood, and fire companies were often organized early in response to this danger. This fire engine was photographed at the corner of Monterey and Chorro in the late 1800s. Courtesy, San Luis Obispo County Historical Museum

own use, or for sale as brightly painted souvenirs of the mission. Without these tiles the adobe deteriorated rapidly. The support beams began to rot, until the heavy Peruvian bells could no longer be enclosed in the arched campanile over the entrance. They had to be moved to a separate New England-style belltower.

In 1875 Father Apollinarius Rouselle was forced to hire William Evans, a skilled carpenter from Kansas, to reface the outside walls of the mission with clapboard. What a strange merging—Mediterranean-style adobe with Yankee clapboard! The clapboard was milled in Redwood City and shipped from there to Port Harford (now Port San Luis). This strange combination kept the building dry and permitted its continued use as a church for a growing parish.

Unfortunately the clapboard

Left: The disastrous fire of 1920 in Mission San Luis Obispo revealed the need for extensive renovation. Father Daniel Keenan founded the community celebration "La Fiesta de Las Flores" in 1925 to raise funds for this work. A major source of funding for the renovation efforts in the 1920s and 1930s was William Randolph Hearst. Courtesy, Old Mission Parish

Right: This painting was ordered for Mission San Luis Obispo by Father Serra in 1774. He purchased the painting in Mexico and paid 18 pesos for it. When Serra offered the painting to the Mission, Father Caveller tactfully requested that the painting be offered to another mission. Serra eventually took the painting to Mission Carmel. The painting eventually came to Mission San Luis Obispo in the late 1890s. Courtesy, San Luis Obispo County Historical Museum

Bottom: Since the early days of the mission era, the Catholic tradition has greatly influenced the county. This is the Catholic church in Nipomo, photographed circa 1915. Courtesy, Rizzie Porter Phelan

Top: As mayor of San Luis Obispo for 20 years (1919 to 1939), Louis F. Sinsheimer supported restoration of the mission. He was also involved with the family store, the Sinsheimer Brothers, for many years. The store is still a landmark in San Luis Obispo. Courtesy, San Luis Obispo County Historical Museum, Sinsheimer Family Collection

Bottom: In 1905 San Luis Obispo's new Carnegie-funded library opened to the public. This view of the library was taken before 1910, when a porch was added to the building. This served as the city's library for 50 years, until 1955. In 1956 it became the San Luis Obispo County Historical Museum. Courtesy, San Luis Obispo County Historical Museum

did permit some moisture to leak under its surface and into the adobe. During hot summer afternoons this presented a problem similar to that caused by storing large quantities of moist rags in an attic space: spontaneous combustion.

Numerous mysterious fires plagued the mission during the early years of the twentieth century. Poorly wired lighting fixtures may have led to the nearly disastrous fire of March 27, 1920. The fire destroyed the roof of the church. A good deal of the old roof was composed of tules and reeds woven by the neophytes more than a century earlier. The flames had smoldered for hours until they were discovered by

a lamplighter, who was making his early morning rounds, turning off the gaslights which illuminated the streets of San Luis Obispo. Ironically, the 120-year-old oak rafters—hand-hewn by the neophytes with hoe-like axes called adzes, and tied in place with rawhide thongs—held in place. They alone prevented the adobe walls from collapsing.

Just before the roof caved in, Father Bernard Dolan, the curate, heroically ran into the blazing structure to save the Blessed Sacrament. Although damaged from water and smoke, the ancient altar and much of the sacristy—where the fire may have begun—were saved.

The statues of the Blessed Virgin, Saint Louis of Toulouse—patron saint of the mission and of the city named after it—and Saint Anthony of Padua were saved along with most of the paintings. A campaign to raise $70,000 to restore the mission was announced later that Saturday morning by Louis Sinsheimer, the mayor of San Luis Obispo.

The funds were sufficient to put the church back in working order with a new roof, but architectural experts said that the clapboard had to be removed and the adobe walls reconstructed to ensure the building's permanency. In the meantime an epidemic of hoof-and-mouth disease had struck the region's dairy and cattle industry, creating a local financial crisis. It would be next to impossible to raise the funds needed for restoring the mission without outside help. The matching funds

for historic preservation from state bond acts, the like of which recently helped save the porch from collapse at the County Museum—the 1904 Carnegie Library—were unavailable.

Father Daniel Keenan, the energetic pastor of the Old Mission from 1925 to 1929, provided the initial basis for such funds when he founded *La Fiesta de las Flores* (The Festival of Flowers) in 1925. Keenan fully understood the potential of "mission mania" as an attraction in the age of the automobile.

Keenan advertised in *Touring Topics,* now called *Westways,* the magazine of the Automobile Club of Southern California; *The Tidings,* the widely circulated newspaper of the Archdiocese of Los Angeles; the *Los Angeles Times,* in Bill Henry's popular column; and over radio stations in San Jose and Los Angeles, including Earl C. An-

Top: The San Luis Obispo County Historical Society was founded in 1953. In this photo, Pearl and A.E. "Mike" Mallagh are manning an early society booth. The Mallaghs were among those instrumental in forming the society. Courtesy, San Luis Obispo County Historical Museum

Bottom: San Luis Obispo's Chinatown played a part in community celebrations. The building shown behind this float from the 1928 La Fiesta Parade later became widely known as Chong's Candy Store. Courtesy, San Luis Obispo County Historical Museum

Top: Camp San Luis Obispo hosted nearly 500,000 troops at a rate of 10,000 at a time. This massive influx of population included many who decided that this was a place in which they wanted to live. This is the first troop train arriving in April 1941. Courtesy, San Luis Obispo County Historical Museum

Bottom: Camp San Luis Obispo grew from a summer training camp of the California National Guard into one of the largest U.S. army training camps in the States during 1941-1942. This view shows the camp around 1943 when it was training 10,000 men every two months. Courtesy, San Luis Obispo County Historical Museum

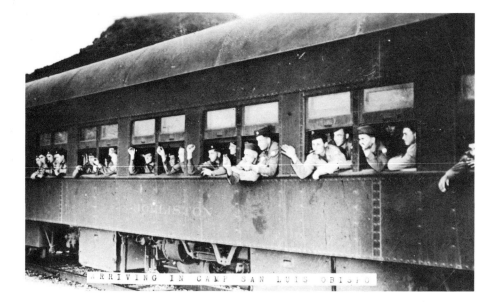

thony's powerful KECA, and later, KFI. Keenan and his successors, Father James Buckley and Father John Francis Harnett, attracted thousands of motorists to the local fiesta.

Keenan used the funds generated by the popular barbecue to pay for the building of Mission High School, now Mission College Preparatory, on Palm Street. The school was located on part of the original mission lands, restored to the Catho-

lic Church by the United States Land Commission in 1855. The surplus, and future profits from La Fiesta, went to the restoration of the mission.

Because of the nationwide Great Depression, funds were not sufficient to begin work until 1934. Under Harnett's direction, the clapboard was taken down from throughout the setting. The area below, now used as museum space, was the priests' quarters until 1963, so

Top: San Luis Obispo was not the only city in the county affected by World War II. The army built a recreational camp near Pismo Beach. Courtesy, San Luis Obispo County Historical Museum

Bottom: The army recreational center near Pismo Beach was a popular retreat for servicemen lucky enough to go there. Though the camp no longer exists, some of the structures are still standing in the south county. Courtesy, San Luis Obispo County Historical Museum

Betty Kurokawa and her daughter are shown here circa 1943 at Fort Snelling, Minnesota. Paul Kurokawa, former student body vice president and athletic star at San Luis Obispo High School, was a language instructor at the now well-known Military Intelligence Language School in Minnesota during World War II. He trained MacArthur's "eyes and ears," proving, as with so many other Japanese, his loyalty to the United States. Courtesy, San Luis Obispo County Historical Museum

been covered with clapboard since the 1870s, and the adobe underneath was in an appalling state of decay. But despite its deteriorated condition, it contained some very special aspects of the history of the region.

In 1936 Father Harnett found some malvaceous seeds, related to wild rose or hollyhock, in the old adobe. He sent these seeds, which had to be at least 130 years old, to Dr. Charles Lipman, Dean of the Graduate School of Agriculture of the University of California. Lipman was anxious to test a theory proposed by Dr. Ira Bartle, a physician-scientist, that soil bacteria continue to live in a state of suspended animation. Bartle was interested in the medical benefits that might emerge from such knowledge.

Lipman was able to grow a mature plant from the mallow seeds sent to him from the old adobe wall. He reported on this in scientific journals, which prompted the Field Museum of Natural History in Chicago to send Bartle some seeds from lotus plants found buried under 200-year-old peat deposits in Manchuria. Bartle also reported receiving 2,000-year-old bacteria samples from ancient ruins in Honduras. Thus Harnett's seed discovery in the Old Mission walls furthered medical research and resulted in national news bylines in late June 1938.

Harnett, who suffered from a lengthy illness, died in St. Vincent's Hospital in Los Angeles on July 3, 1939. With his death, most of the restoration work came to a standstill.

no other area was available. The mission was appropriately in situ, beneath the tile-covered tules of the ancient roof. Harnett had planned to move the museum downstairs, but that was not possible in his lifetime. Yet the public loved the museum, which opened in 1934. It became a major attraction of that year's La Fiesta de las Flores on June 8, 9, and 10.

The stripping down of the Old Mission yielded a variety of secrets. The structure had

War clouds loomed over the world for the next eight years. San Luis Obispo busied itself, preparing to receive 40,000 trainees at the newly constructed Camp San Luis. Construction materials and labor were not available for civilian projects such as the restoration of the Old Mission.

Within a year the entire Central Coast region had begun to prepare for wartime mobilization. The construction of camps Cook, San Luis, and Roberts, along with various Army Air Corps and Naval facilities at Santa Maria, Paso Robles, and Morro Bay, drained the supply of labor and materials. The Old Mission would have to wait for the Allied victory over the Axis powers before basic needs could once again be met.

By 1946 these needs were once again as critical as they had been at the time of the disastrous fire in 1920. The Archdiocese of San Francisco and the Diocese of Monterey-Fresno had been given large sums of money by wealthy donors, including William Randolph Hearst, to rebuild the Franciscan missions in their respective jurisdictions. Bishop Joseph McGucken, acting administrator for the Monterey-Fresno Diocese, then contacted Harry Downie, restorer of the Carmel mission. Because some of the mission restoration funding was needed to pay off pressing diocesan debts, a prioritized schedule for restorations was developed.

Work on the Old Mission did not resume until the autumn of 1947. The new pastor,

Monsignor Patrick Daly, undertook a vigorous program of restoration and enlargement. The stubby "L" addition of 1893 was extended to the edge of Chorro Street, nearly doubling the size of the church. The remnants of the quadrangle's southwest wall were taken out, and a new convent and chapel for the Immaculate Heart Sisters was constructed along the Broad Street side. These now serve as the parish school and senior citizens center.

Missions San Antonio, near Jolon, and San Juan Bautista, near Hollister, were in extremely run-down condition, requiring immediate restoration if they were to be saved. Mission Soledad, just northwest of the town of Soledad, was in ruins and needed complete rebuilding. Mission San Luis Obispo, the most actively used parish along the Central Coast, still had not recovered from the 1920 fire. Bishop McGucken sent Downie to San Luis Obispo with a promise of $50,000 in funding.

Downie later reported that these promised funds initially created considerable tension between himself and Daly. The fiscally prudent monsignor had to pay the restoration bills out of his own parish funds until the check from the diocese came. By that time he had spent approximately $45,000. In later years Downie would laugh, saying that the minute he presented the check to Daly, they became great friends. Up until that moment, however, a stony wall of silence existed between these

two strong-willed Irishmen.

Downie recalled that "rats and mice were his constant companions in the restoration task." The mission structures, after all, had been used for just about every conceivable purpose for nearly 150 years: church, barn, schoolhouse, courtroom, jail, prison, hospital, charnel house, bottle shop, parish meeting place, rectory, and museum.

He began his task by pulling up the old wooden floors installed during the mid-1870s. Much to his surprise, he found that the original floors were made not of the typical mission tile, but rather of *mescal*, a hand-laid cement made from lime and given a pinkish color through the addition of cinnabar (mercury ore). Downie replaced it with a modern cement floor having similar color. He planned to set pipes in the cement for radiant heating, saying "This will make San Luis Obispo one of the most comfortable missions in California." Unfortunately, Downie's plans for heating were not entirely fulfilled, as they were too costly and would have interfered with the function of the pews.

Downie found that many of the exterior walls of the mission contained underlayers of limestone plaster colored with cinnabar. Several early travelers had reported that the mission once had red walls. These accounts were discounted at the time, regarded as the effects of sunset, faulty eyesight, or memory. Nowadays mission scholars speculate on the reasons for the red walls, some theorizing that they were designed to absorb rather than reflect heat, the way whitewashed plaster might.

The original mission did not have pews; it had only a few benches scattered throughout the church. As a result, there had been many accessible niches for holy water and shrines. When the pews were nailed in place, these niches evidently were plastered over. Fragments of the dishes that the padres used—made in China and shipped to California from the Philippine trade—were found in the decaying plaster over the niches.

Downie found a large niche, corresponding to a baptismal font area, on the east side of the main wall. Today this niche, located near the rear of the church, is used for the illuminated shrine to "Our Lady, Refuge of Sinners." Downie also found the remains of a door leading to the Indian graveyard, which stretched out to what is today Chorro Street.

The 40-foot-long "L" extension toward Chorro Street, completed in 1893, was extended by another 40 feet in 1948. Downie found many Indian artifacts and remains under the most recent section. The artifacts were placed in the Mission Museum, and the remains were sent to the Lowie Museum of Anthropology at the University of California at Berkeley. Under today's laws they would have been disposed of according to the instructions of a Native American archaeological observer, now required at all sensitive sites.

The original interior walls were whitewashed plaster with a 22-inch-high border of ocher color reaching up from the floor. This was capped at the periphery with a two-inch wide cinnabar line. At some points, beautiful classical designs were found painted on a lavender background. Downie believed these to be the work of Esteban Munras, a Catalonian artisan who came from Spain to California in 1818. Munras also did the beautiful painting at Mission San Miguel. Munras Street in Monterey is named after him.

Downie completely redid the altar area. At first he was puzzled by the padres' ability to simulate the green shades of *verde antique* marble on wood, the style of the present altar. After a number of attempts to simulate the surface color and texture of this type of marble—unavailable in California—Downie learned the secret. Gregorio Silverio, the bell ringer whose grandfather had been taught how to ring bells by the padres, reportedly said "They painted the wood with turkey feathers, Mr. Downie." Harry Downie got some turkey feathers from a farm near Santa Margarita, and they did the job!

Today the mission combines the authentic aesthetics of the church as it appeared in about 1820 with the functionalism necessary for modern liturgies, and happily serves to unite all of the various eras—Native American, Hispanic, and American—as we look backward into the Middle Kingdom.

PART TWO

Modern-Day San Luis Obispo

The Port San Luis Light-
house was a popular out-
ing destination around
the turn of the century.
Courtesy, San Luis
Obispo County Histori-
cal Museum

Port San Luis has been the county's main shipping terminus since the mission era. It is still home to a fishing fleet and the Union Oil shipping facilities. Photo by Tim Olson

Top: The Sebastian Store in San Simeon boasts of having served many of William Randolph Hearst's guests when they were staying "on the hill" or "at the ranch." It is still in operation today, catering to visitors to Hearst's Castle. Photo by Tim Olson

Bottom: Ah Louis built this store out of bricks produced in his own brickyard during the 1870s. It is still in operation, run by his son and daughter-in-law. Photo by Tim Olson

Bishop's Peak was so named because the rocks on top were said to resemble a bishop's mitre. Photo by Tim Olson

Top: This tallow pot at the Dana Adobe in Nipomo was used during the nineteenth century. The cattle industry thrived on the rolling hills of Nipomo. Photo by Tim Olson

Bottom: Wine making was founded in California by the mission fathers. The industry experienced a rebirth during the 1970s and is a major industry today. Photo by Tim Olson

Top: The San Luis Obispo Criterium is an annual bike race which attracts athletes from all over the world. Photo by Tim Olson

Bottom: The 1942 Fremont Theater is one of downtown San Luis Obispo's noted landmarks. Photo by Tim Olson

Top: Lopez Lake is a favorite vacation area for residents and visitors alike. Photo by Tim Olson

Bottom: Montana de Oro State Park offers spectacular seaside vistas to the casual visitor or hiker. Photo by R. Dana Holt

Top: Pismo Beach has been a popular recreational location since the late-nineteenth century. Photo by Tim Olson

Bottom: Avila Beach, well noted for its wide, sandy beach, has been a tourist destination for 100 years. Photo by R. Dana Holt

BIBLIOGRAPHY

CHAPTER I

Blackburn, Thomas C. *December's Child: A Book of Chumash Oral Narratives.* Berkeley and Los Angeles: University of California Press, 1975.

Boneu Companys, F. *Gaspar de Portola: Explorer and Founder of California.* Translated and revised by Alan K. Brown. Lerida, Spain: Instituto de Estudios Ilerdenses, 1983.

Careri, Giovanni Franceso Gemelli. "Narrative of a Voyage of a Spanish Galleon from Manila to Acapulco in 1687-1688." *Churchill's Collection of Voyages and Travels* (translation), volume 4. London: 1752.

Heizer, Robert F. "Archaeological Evidence of Sebastian Rodriguez Cermenho's California Visit." *California Historical Society Quarterly,* volume 20 (December 1941): 315-28.

Holmes, Maurice G. *From New Spain by Sea to the Californias, 1519-1668.* Glendale, California: Arthur H. Clark Company, 1963.

Kelsey, Harry. *Juan Rodriguez Cabrillo.* San Marino, California: The Huntington Library, 1986.

Mathes, Michael W. *Vizcaino and Spanish Exploration in the Pacific Ocean, 1580-1630.* San Francisco: California Historical Society, 1968.

Moratto, Michael J., Thomas F. King, and Wallace B. Woolfenden. "Archaeology and California's Climate." *Journal of California Anthropology,* volume 5 (Winter 1978): 151-160.

Shurz, William L. *The Manila Galleon.* New York: 1939.

Squibb, Paul. *Captain Portola in San Luis Obispo County in 1769: Portions of the Diary of Fr. Juan Crespi, O.F.M., as edited and augmented from other diaries by his colleague, Fr. Francisco Palou.* Spanish translations, corrections, and revisions by Herbert E. Bolton, with further revisions by Alan K. Brown and introduction by Dan Krieger. Morro Bay, California: Tabula Rasa Press, 1984.

Wagner, Henry R. "Spanish Voyages to the Northwest Coast of America in the Sixteenth Century." *Society Quarterly,* vol 3 (April 1924): 3-24.

. *Cartography of the Northwest Coast of America to the year 1800.* 2 volumes (1937).

. *The Voyage to California of Sebastian Rodriguez Cermenho in 1595.* California Historical Society, 1931.

CHAPTER II

Bancroft, Hubert Howe. *The Works of Hubert Howe Bancroft, vol. 18: The History of California, Volume I: 1542-1800.* San Francisco: H.H. Bancroft Co., 1884.

Cameron, William R. "Rancho Santa Margarita." *California Historical Society Quarterly,* (March 1957).

Cook, S.F. "Smallpox in Spanish and Mexican California, 1770-1845." *Bulletin of the History of Medicine,* volume 7 (1939): 1453-1491.

. *The Conflict Between the California Indian and White Civilization.* Berkeley and Los Angeles: University of California Press, 1976.

Englehardt, Zephyrin, O.F.M. *Missions and Missionaries of California,* volume 2, chapter 18. San Francisco: James H. Barry, Company: 1908-1916.

. *Mission San Carlos Borromeo.* Santa Barbara: Mission Santa Barbara Press, 1934.

. *Mission San Luis Obispo in the Valley of the Bears.* Santa Barbara: Franciscan Fathers of California, 1933.

Fages, Pedro. *A Historical, Political and Natural Description of California by Pedro Fages.* Berkeley: University of California Press, 1937.

. *Informe Sobre Missiones,* no. 26, MSS, Bancroft Library.

Font, Pedro, O.F.M. *Anza's California Expeditions,* volume 4. Translated and edited by Herbert Eugene Bolton. Berkeley: University of California Press, 1930.

Nuttall, Donald. "Pedro Fages and the Advance of the Northern Frontier of New Spain." Ph.D. dissertation, MSS, University of Southern California, 1964.

Palou, Francisco. *Historical Memoirs of New California by Fray Francisco Palou, O.F.M.* Translated and edited from the MSS in the archives of Mexico by Herbert Eugene Bolton. Boston: Atheneum House, 1926.

. *Palou's Life of Fray Junipero Serra.* Translated and annotated by Maynard J. Geiger, O.F.M. Washington, D.C.: Academy of American Franciscan History, 1955.

Tibesar, Antonine, O.F.M. *The Writings of Junipero Serra,* volume 4. Washington: Franciscan Society of America, 1966, 327-329.

Valle, Rosemary K. "Prevention of Smallpox in Alta California During the Franciscan Mission Period (1769-1833)." *California Medicine,* volume 119 (1973): 73-77.

Webb, Edith B. *Indian Life at the Old Missions.* Los Angeles: Dawson Books, 1952.

CHAPTER III

Angel, Myron. *History of San Luis Obispo County, California; with Illustrations and Biographical Sketches of its Prominent Men and Pioneers.* Oakland: Thompson and West, 1883.

Bancroft, Hubert Howe. *California Pastorale.* San Francisco: A.L. Bancroft, 1888.

. *History of California,* volume 3 (1824-1840) in *The Works of Hubert Howe Bancroft,* volume 20. San Francisco: The History Company, 1886.

Bell, Horace. *Reminiscences of a Ranger or Early Times in Southern California.* Los Angeles: 1881.

Bell, Katherine M. *Swinging the Censer: Reminiscences of Old Santa Barbara.* Santa Barbara: 1931.

Blomquist, Leonard Rudolph. "A Regional Study of the Changes in Life and Institutions in the San Luis Obispo District, 1830 to 1850." M.A. thesis. University of California, Berkeley, 1943.

Boessenecker, John. "Pio Linares: Californio Bandido." *The Californians,* volume 5, no. 6 (November/December 1987): 34-44.

Bonilla, Jose Mariano. *Documentos para la Historia de California, 1807-1898.* Collected by H.H. Bancroft. MSS. The Bancroft Library, University of California, Berkeley.

Branch, Francis Ziba. Correspondence and Papers. MSS. The Bancroft Library, University of California, Berkeley.

Brooks, Benjamin Hassen. Recollections. MSS (c. 1925). The Bancroft Library, University of California, Berkeley.

Bryant, Edwin. *What I Saw in California.* Philadelphia: G. Appleton & Sons, 1848; Lincoln and London: University of Nebraska Bison Books, 1985.

Cameron, William R. "Rancho Santa Margarita of San Luis Obispo." *California Historical Society Quarterly,* volume 36, no. 1 (March 1957): 1-24.

Caughey, John W. *Hubert Howe Bancroft, Historian of the West.* Berkeley and Los Angeles: University of California Press, 1946.

Cowan, Robert G. *Ranchos of California: A List of Spanish . . . and Mexican Grants . . .* Los Angeles:

The Historical Society of Southern California, 1977.

Crosby, Elisha Oscar. *Memoirs of Elisha Oscar Crosby: reminiscences of California and Guatemala from 1849 to 1864.* Edited by Charles Albro Barker. San Marino: Huntington Library, 1945.

Dally, Harry J. Memoirs dictated to E.F. Murray for H.H. Bancroft in 1878. MSS. The Bancroft Library, University of California, Berkeley.

Dana, Juan Francisco. *The Blond Ranchero: Memories of Juan Francisco Dana as told to Rocky Dana and Marie Harrington.* Los Angeles: Dawson's Book Shop, 1960.

Dana, Richard Henry. *Two Years Before the Mast.* London: J.M. Dent & Sons, Ltd., "Everyman's Library" edition, 1912: 67.

Dart, Louisiana Clayton. *What's in a Name?* San Luis Obispo: Mission Federal Savings, 1979: 4.

Engelhardt, Zephyrin. *San Miguel Archangel: The Mission on the Highway.* Santa Barbara: Mission Santa Barbara Press, 1929.

Fremont, John C. *Memoirs of My Life,* volume I. Chicago and New York: Belford and Company, 1887.

Garcia, Innocente. *Hechos.* MSS: 68-70. The Bancroft Library, University of California, Berkeley.

Genini, Ronald, and Richard Hitchman. *Romualdo Pacheco: A Californio in Two Eras.* San Francisco: The Book Club of California, 1985.

Harloe, Leo Marcus. *The Life of Isaac J. Sparks.* M.A. thesis. University of Southern California, 1948.

Kocher, Paul H. *Mission San Luis Obispo de Tolosa: A Historical Sketch.* San Luis Obispo: Blake Printing & Publishing, Inc., 1972.

Leonard, Ralph J. *John Michael Price: A California Ranchero.* San Luis Obispo: Self-published, 1981; reprinted by the San Luis Obispo County Historical Society and the South (San Luis Obispo) County Historical Society, 1987.

. "The San Miguel Mission Murders." *La Vista,* volume 4, no. 1 (June 1980): 18-29.

Lynch, James. *With Stevenson to California.* San Luis Obispo: Biobooks, 1954.

Maclean, Angus. *Legends of the California Bandidos.* San Luis Obispo: Padre Press, 1976.

Moes, Robert J. "Smallpox Immunization in Alta California: A Story Based On Jose Estrada's 1821 Postscript." *Southern California Quarterly,* volume 61, no. 2 (Summer 1979).

Mofras, Eugene Duflot de. *Exploration du territoire de l'Oregon, des Californies et de la mer Vermeille executee pendant les annees 1840, 1841 et 1842,* volume I: 320. Paris: Arthus Bertrand, editeur, 1844.

Murray, Walter and Alexander. The Murray Family Papers, 1843-1889. Includes transcript of letters by Dorothy Unangst Bilodeau. MSS. The Bancroft Library, University of California, Berkeley.

Nicholson, Loren. "Captain John Wilson: Trader of the Pacific." *The Pacific Historian,* volume 23, no. 2 (Summer 1979): 69-90.

Pico, Jose de Jesus. *Acontecimientos en California.* Dictation taken by Thomas Savage for H.H. Bancroft on April 22, 1878. MSS. The Bancroft Library, University of California, Berkeley.

Robinson, Alfred. *Life in California During a Residence of Several Years in that Territory.* Introduction by Andrew Rolle. Including Reverend Geronimo Boscana's *Chinigchinich: An Historical Account of the Origin, Customs, and Traditions of the Indians of Alta-California.* Santa Barbara and

Salt Lake City: Peregrine Publishers, Inc., 1970.

Ross, Dudley T. *Devil on Horseback: A Biography of "Notorious" Jack Powers.* Fresno: Valley Publishers, 1975.

Savage, Thomas. "Reports of Labors on Archives and Procuring Materials for History of California," 1876-79. MSS. The Bancroft Library, University of California, Berkeley.

Streeter, William A. "Memoirs of William A. Streeter." Edited by William A. Ellison. *California Historical Society Quarterly,* (March, June, and September 1939).

Tays, George. "Revolutionary California: The Political History of California During the Mexican Period, 1822-1846." Ph.D. dissertation. MSS. University of California, Berkeley, 1932.

Vallejo, Mariano G. *Historia de California.* Vallejo MSS, vol. 2: 96-100. The Bancroft Library, University of California, Berkeley.

CHAPTER IV

Brooks, Benjamin. "Recollections" (c. 1925). MSS. The Bancroft Library, University of California, Berkeley.

"El Paso de Robles." *Los Angeles Tribune,* April 13, 1887.

Evans, John. *Agriculture in San Luis Obispo County.* San Luis Obispo: Agricultural Extension, University of California, 1979.

Fisher, Ann Benson. *The Salinas: Upside Down River.* Fresno: Valley Publishers, 1945, 1971.

Gates, Dorothy L. and Jan Horton Bailey. *Morro Bay's Yesterdays: Vignettes of Our City's Lives & Times.* Morro Bay: El Moro Publications, 1982.

Giffen, Helen S. "An Adopted California." *Historical Society of Southern California Quarterly,* volume 19 (1937).

. *Casas and Courtyards: Historic Adobe Houses of California.* Oakland: Biobooks, 1955.

. "Some Early Two-Story Adobe Houses of Early California." *Historical Society of Southern California Quarterly,* volume 20 (1938).

Gilfillian, Josephine. *Templeton: Today and Yesterday.* Paso Robles: Paso Robles Press, 1965.

Graves, William J. *California Road Laws in Force in San Luis Obispo County.* San Francisco: A.L. Bancroft and Co., 1874.

Guinn, J.M. *History of the State of California and Biographical Record of Coast Counties. An Historical Survey of the State's Growth from its Earliest Settlement to the Present Time, Containing the Biographies of Well Known Citizens, Past and Present.* Chicago: Chapman Publishing Co., 1904.

Halterman, John Frederick. *Economic Development in San Luis Obispo County and the Western Part of Santa Barbara County.* Santa Barbara: 1949.

Hamilton, Geneva. *Where the Highway Ends.* Cambria: Williams Printing Co., 1974.

Jesperson, Christian Nelson and Audrey V. Kell, et al. *History of San Luis Obispo County.* San Luis Obispo: H.M. Meier, 1939.

Lamb, Frank W. *San Simeon: A Brief History.* Fullerton, California: Sultana Press, 1971.

Lewis, William H. *Atascadero Colony Days.* Atascadero: The Treasure of El Camino Real, 1974.

Mackey, Marge. *Recalling Atascadero, California.* Atascadero: The Treasure of El Camino Real, 1980.

Maclean, Angus. "The Legend of Frank and Jesse James in Paso Robles and La Panza." *La Vista,* volume 1, no. 1 (July 1968): 42-46.

Morrison, Annie L. *History of San Luis Obispo County and its Environs.* Los Angeles: Historic Record Co., 1917.

Morse, Malcolm. *A Treatise on the Hot Sulphur Springs . . . Paso Robles, California.* San Francisco: Eaton & Edwards, 1874.

. *Hot Springs.* San Francisco: A. Roman & Company, 1869.

Newmark, Marco. "Early California Resorts." *The Historical Society of Southern California Quarterly,* volume 35 (June 1953).

Nicholson, Loren. *Rails Across the Ranchos.* Fresno: Valley Publishers, 1980.

Ochs, Patricia Mary. "Chinese in San Luis Obispo." *La Vista,* volume 2, no. 1 (June 1970).

Phillips, Chauncy Hatch, et al. *The Resources and Attractions of San Luis Obispo, California.* San Luis Obispo: Tribune Publishing Co., 1887.

Robinson, William Wilcox. *Lands in California: The Story of the Mission Lands, Ranch Squatters, Mining Claims, Railroad Grants, Landscript, Homesteads.* Berkeley: University of California Press, 1948.

San Luis Obispo County Telegram-Tribune. Centurama: 100 Years of Progress--San Luis Obispo, 1856-1956. San Luis Obispo: Tribune Publishing Co., 1956.

Shinn, Charles Howard. *A Study of San Luis Obispo, California.* San Luis Obispo: San Luis Obispo Board of Trade, 1901.

Sinnard, L.G. "The Garden of the Bishop: A Study of the Characteristics of San Luis Obispo County, California." *Sunset* (March 1904).

Stern, Norton B. "The Sinsheimers of San Luis Obispo." *Western States Jewish Historical Quarterly* (October 1973).

Vachell, Horace Annesley. *Life and Sport on the Pacific Slope.* London: 1900.

Van Harreveld, Constance. "Adobe Diary." *La Vista,* volume 3, no. 5 (1975).

Waltz, Marcus L. "Chronicles of Cambria's Pioneers." *The Cambrian* (1946).

CHAPTER V

Angel, Myron. *History of San Luis Obispo County.* Oakland: Thompson and West, 1883.

Avila, Miguel. *Notas Californias.* MSS. The Bancroft Library, University of California, Berkeley.

Bancroft, Hubert Howe. *History of California, volume II, 1801-1824.* San Francisco: The History Company, 1886.

Best, Gerald. *Ships and Narrow Gauge Rails.* Berkeley: Howell-North Publications, 1964.

Brown, Patrick. Quoted in Dan Krieger, "Times Past: Oil Comes to SLO." *San Luis Obispo County Telegram-Tribune* (March 31, 1984).

Cooley, Ethel. "Fast Wheeling in the Motor Corps." *La Vista,* volume 4, no. 2 (1981, 1982): 20.

Engelhardt, Zephyrin. *Mission San Luis Obispo in the Valley of the Bears.* Santa Barbara: W.T. Genns, 1933, 1963.

Hess, Chester Norton. "What California Means to Its Oldest Chinese." *Westways,* volume 26, No. 3 (March 1934): 26-40.

Krieger, Dan. "Narrow Gauge Relic Found A Home at Old S.L.O. Adobe." "Times Past" feature in *San Luis Obispo County Telegram Tribune* (August 2, 1986.)

. "Narrow Rails and Coasting Cars Helped Build S.L.O." "Times Past" feature in *San Luis Obispo County Telegram Tribune* (July 12, 1986.)

McElwain, Alan. "The Quiet Nook of Avila Beach." *Chevron U.S.A.* (Spring 1970).

Melendy, H. Brett. "One Hundred Years of the Redwood Lumber Industry, 1850-1950." Ph.D. dissertation, Stanford University, 1952.

Miossi, Harold. "Somnolent Cape: The Story of the Pecho Coast." *La Vista,* volume 3, no. 2: 1-31.

Pomeroy, Earl. *The Pacific Slope.* Seattle: University of Washington Press, 1965.

Robinson, Alfred. *Life in California.* Santa Barbara and Salt Lake City: Peregrine Publishers, Inc., 1851, 1971.

Robinson, William Wilcox. *The Story of San Luis Obispo County.* Los Angeles: Title Insurance Co., 1957, 1962.

San Luis Obispo Tribune. San Luis Obispo. February 23, 1883; October 11, 29, 1883; November 15, 1883; April 16, 1908.

The Daily Republic. San Luis Obispo. May 21, 1887; October 4, 1887; December 12, 26, 1887; August 25, 1888; September 15, 1888.

Welty, Earl M., and Frank J. Taylor. *The "76" Bonanza: The Fabulous Life and Times of the Union Oil Company of California.* Menlo Park, California: Lane Magazine and Book Co., 1966.

White, Gerald. *Formative Years in the Far West: A History of the Standard Oil Company of California and Predecessors through 1919.* New York: Appleton, Century, Crofts, 1962.

Yale, Charles G. *Pacific Coast Harbors.* San Francisco: 1879.

CHAPTER VI

Angel, Myron. *History of the California Polytechnic School at San Luis Obispo, California.* San Luis Obispo: 1908.

Black, Mary Gail. *Profile of the Daily Telegram: A Story of San Luis Obispo, 1921-1923.* San Luis Obispo: Tabula Rasa Press, 1988.

Coffman, Taylor. *Hearst Castle: The Story of William Randolph Hearst and San Simeon.* Santa Barbara: Sequoia Books, 1986.

Hannum, Anna P., ed. *A Quaker Forty-Niner: The Adventures of Charles Edward Pancoast on the American Frontier.* Philadelphia: 1930.

Loe, Nancy. *Hearst.* Santa Barbara: Sequoia Books, 1988.

McKeen, Rose Polin. *Parade Along the Creek: San Luis Obispo Memories of the 1920's through '60's.* San Luis Obispo: Self-published, 1988.

Morrison, Annie M. *A Historical Sketch of the California State Polytechnic School: 1903-1933.* San Luis Obispo: 1934.

Smith, Morris Eugene. "History of California State Polytechnic: The First Fifty Years: 1901-1951." Ed.D. thesis. MSS. University of Oregon, Eugene, 1957.

Sutherland, Sidney S. *A History of Agricultural Education in the Schools of California, 1910 to 1940.* San Luis Obispo: California State Commission for Agricultural Education, 1940.

CHAPTER VII

Krieger, Dan. Interview with Harry Downie. Carmel, California. May 19, 1965.

Kocher, Paul H. *Mission San Luis Obispo de Tolosa: A Historical Sketch.* San Luis Obispo: Blake Printing Company, 1972.

San Luis Obispo County Telegram. San Luis Obispo. March 20, 21, 1920.

San Luis Obispo Morning Tribune. San Luis Obispo. March 20, 21, 1920.

The Tidings. (Official newspaper of the Archdiocese of Los Angeles) March 20, 21, 1920.

Weber, Francis J. *Mission in the Valley of the Bears: A Documentary History of Mission San Luis Obispo de Tolosa.* San Fernando, California: Monsignor Francis J. Weber, Archives of the Archdiocese of Los Angeles, 1985.

INDEX